FOR ALL OF THE RELATIVES OF KYR,
AND THOSE NAMED FOR HIM.

WAR LETTERS

OF

KIFFIN YATES ROCKWELL

Foreign Legionnaire and Aviator
France, 1914 – 1916

WITH MEMOIR AND NOTES BY

PAUL AYRES ROCKWELL

LETTER TO THE READER

SHANE KIFFIN AYERS

War Letters of Kiffin Yates Rockwell
First Printed in 1925
Doubleday, Page & Company
The Country Life Press
Garden City, NY
By Paul Ayres Rockwell,
Author and Brother of Kiffin Yates Rockwell

House of Ayers-Ayres Edtion 2008
with the addition of "Letter to the Reader"
By Shane Kiffin Ayers

ISBN 978-0-615-25307-7

Dear Reader,

I hope your journey finds you in a great condition. If you are weary, then Thank You for taking the time to read a bit of this notable history. If you are solidly abiding and strong to your journey's call, then Thank You too and may you be encouraged to continue your bravery toward life.

We all find ourselves wondering what things or events were like in history. It is always wonderful to read a firsthand account of any experience. War is a rough experience that should be wished on no one, but as history tells we are faced with these realities.

The intent of this book is to fly us back to a time that many will never know, and those who remember it are the ones encapsulated in a work such as this.

Immortality may not be the intent of any true Hero, but heroism has a way of being immortalized. The stories we tell, the movies we enjoy, and the relatives we honor are all part of our hero's journey. It may not mean that they were perfect, or were always successful. It will mean however that their part in the larger community of the world was integral in shaping where we are today.

I believe that history appears boring or stale to many because of a lost connection with our dependency to history. There is value in recognizing this connection and great learning from the choices of our collective past that can empower our future. By identifying with our ancestors by name and seeking to understand the world in which they lived, we are participating today in an effort that can bring reconciliation to a world community that longs to identify with humanity.

If I die, you will know that I die as every man should—in fighting for the right. I do not consider that I am fighting for France alone, but for the cause of humanity, the most noble of all causes.

The aforementioned quote is for me the most prominent quote of Kiffin Yates Rockwell. It gives a glimpse of his raw passion and genuine respect for others. It is hard to compare people like Kiffin, but I believe that everyone who rises to a challenge and stands in the face of adversity becomes a Hero to someone who needs one.

Rising to the Occasion,

Shalom,

S.K. Ayers

P. S.

Enjoy these letters and writings for what they are, a glimpse into the past. Kiffin's letters were written from 1914 to 1916, and published by Paul Ayres Rockwell, P.A.R., in 1925. The times and settings were illuminated differently than they are today.

This work is also not to be critiqued for its grammatical content. It is a work of real life, not academic advancement. The English at times is a mixture of British, American and French borrowings. The book as a whole is to be viewed as a counterpart to all of the other literature that helps us to understand soldiers in World War I and soldiers in general.

If nothing else is gathered from this book, then gather an understanding of the need to show up where we are needed and support others in our common goal to uphold justice for the world.

Contents

Kiffin Yates Rockwell

Dear Reader,

I hope your journey finds you in a great condition. If you are weary, then Thank You for taking the time to read a bit of this notable history. If you are solidly abiding and strong to your journey's call, then Thank You too and may you be encouraged to continue your bravery toward life.

We all find ourselves wondering what things or events were like in history. It is always wonderful to read a firsthand account of any experience. War is a rough experience that should be wished on no one, but as history tells we are faced with these realities.

The intent of this book is to fly us back to a time that many will never know, and those who remember it are the ones encapsulated in a work such as this.

Immortality may not be the intent of any true Hero, but heroism has a way of being immortalized. The stories we tell, the movies we enjoy, and the relatives we honor are all part of our hero's journey. It may not mean that they were perfect, or were always successful. It will mean however that their part in the larger community of the world was integral in shaping where we are today.

I believe that history appears boring or stale to many because of a lost connection with our dependency to history. There is value in recognizing this connection and great learning from the choices of our collective past that can empower our future. By identifying with our ancestors by name and seeking to understand the world in which they lived, we are participating today in an effort that can bring reconciliation to a world community that longs to identify with humanity.

If I die, you will know that I die as every man should—in fighting for the right. I do not consider that I am fighting for France alone, but for the cause of humanity, the most noble of all causes.

The aforementioned quote is for me the most prominent quote of Kiffin Yates Rockwell. It gives a glimpse of his raw passion and genuine respect for others. It is hard to compare people like Kiffin, but I believe that everyone who rises to a challenge and stands in the face of adversity becomes a Hero to someone who needs one.

Rising to the Occasion,

Shalom,

S.K. Ayers

P. S.

Enjoy these letters and writings for what they are, a glimpse into the past. Kiffin's letters were written from 1914 to 1916, and published by Paul Ayres Rockwell, P.A.R., in 1925. The times and settings were illuminated differently than they are today.

This work is also not to be critiqued for its grammatical content. It is a work of real life, not academic advancement. The English at times is a mixture of British, American and French borrowings. The book as a whole is to be viewed as a counterpart to all of the other literature that helps us to understand soldiers in World War I and soldiers in general.

If nothing else is gathered from this book, then gather an understanding of the need to show up where we are needed and support others in our common goal to uphold justice for the world.

Contents

Kiffin Yates Rockwell

To the Memory of
KIFFIN YATES ROCKWELL
(American Aviator)

You who fought for France with a mystic passion,
Soaring fierce and lonely above the thunder,
Fiery one, aggressor in fifty combats,
Ever the bravest;

We, who knew your look, and the noble sweetness,
All your high disdain for the death you smiled upon,
Bend our thoughts in reverence down before you
— Fallen in beauty.

Paul Scott Mowrer.

FOREWORD

I sincerely thank Mr. Paul Scott Mowrer and Mr. Edgar Lee Masters for permission to reprint their beautiful poems to my brother; Mr. Mowrer and Mr. Victor Lawson for permission to reprint Mr. Mowrer's copyrighted articles, first published by the "Chicago Daily News," and Doubleday, Page & Company for permission to quote passages from James Rogers McConnell's book "Flying For France."

PAUL AYRES ROCKWELL

INTRODUCTION

Biographical Memoir; Sketch from "Official History of Lafayette Flying Corps."

KIFFIN YATES ROCKWELL was born September 20, 1892, at Newport, Tennessee, a picturesque little town spread out along the Pigeon River, in the edge of the Appalachian Mountains. He should have been born in Eastern Carolina, the country of his parents, but following doctor's advice, his father and mother had left the flat and rather malarial region where their families had been installed for generations, and removed to the higher altitude of East Tennessee.

I well remember the first time I saw Kiffin. I was about four years old, and my sister and I had been sent to spend the night with some little friends. When we returned home in the morning, our father took us by the hand and led us into our mother's bedroom to see "the present Dr. Snoddy had brought during the night." As I looked at the tiny red mite my feelings were of pride and pleasure that I had a brother.

When Kiffin was within a few days of being one year old, our father died of typhoid fever, which was very prevalent in Newport that year. With our mother, we three children spent the following winter at our maternal grandparents' place in South Carolina. Kiffin, being then the youngest grandchild, was his grandmother's favorite, and until he was fourteen years old, she insisted on his spending at least half of his time with her. Usually he spent the winters in South Carolina, where the climate during that season was mild and agreeable, and his summers in the cooler, forest-clad mountains of East Tennessee.

The outdoor life on his grandfather's cotton and tobacco plantation was wonderful for the growing youngster, and did much to mould his character.

Best of all for Kiffin was his grandfather, a Southerner of the old school, who had fought through the Confederate War from the beginning until the end. With Lee at Appomattox, in April, 1865, "Marse Enoch," as the Negroes called him, had mounted upon his horse when news of the surrender spread through the ragged little army, and had ridden away to his South Carolina home without waiting to be paroled. It was his boast that he had never surrendered to the "Yankees," had never taken the oath of allegiance to the Federal Government, and that he was "unreconstructed." The paternal grandfather, also a Confederate War veteran, had died almost twenty years before Kiffin was born.

From his grandfather Kiffin heard stories of war, in camp and in battle. The little boy would listen for hours to his grandfather, his great-uncle "Tommie," and other elderly men of the neighborhood recounting their battles, their marches, their sufferings from hunger and cold, and their disappointment and grief over the "Lost Cause," and their struggles after. His imagination and his ambition were constantly fired with desire to shine upon the battlefield for a worthy purpose. He learned also how to handle men. The Negroes, who outnumbered the white people at least five to one in this particular part of South Carolina, under the authority of such men as Enoch Shaw Ayres, had gotten over their unrest and unruliness of the years immediately following the war. The "bad niggers" and the "carpet-baggers" had been driven from the country almost two decades before Kiffin was born, and the blacks remaining, all ex-slaves or children of ex-slaves, were fairly industrious and polite. Cheap education brought to the Negroes of the South by well-intentioned but poorly informed New Englanders had barely begun to poison them.

The region abounded in virgin stands of timber, mostly pine on the uplands and cypress in the swampy lowlands and "islands," and wild life was very plentiful. There were a few deer to be found, and countless rabbits, squirrels, raccoons, opossums, foxes, otters, minks, pole-cats, wild-cats, while alligators frequented the Lumber and Pee Dee rivers, only a few miles away. Mocking birds sang all around the house, and the fields and pine woods teemed with bobwhites and innumerable smaller birds; upon the lakes in the swamps were wood ducks, herons, cranes, and in season many kinds of wild ducks and wild geese. Enterprising lumbermen—whom many people look upon as vandals because of the ruthless and destructive way in which they worked—had not yet come down from the North and cut away the forests, and the Negroes had not begun to buy cheap mail-order shotguns from Chicago with which to massacre beast and bird in and out of season, so as virtually to wipe out game in the South.

Kiffin knew how to handle a gun before he was ten years old, and spent many hours in the woods and swamps shooting bobwhites, hawks, rabbits, squirrels, etc. He was accounted a good shot, and was an excellent fisherman, learning from his grandfather how to hook and land trout, bass, "red-breasts," and other excellent and gamey fish. For his books he did not especially care, although he learned his lessons well and quickly, having a keen and clever mind. His favorite reading were books of travel and adventure, and he fairly revelled in the Henty books and the stories of Captain Mayne Reid. But his best hours were those spent out in the open; he was a good swimmer and an excellent horseman; he was especially fond of mounting a wild and unruly Porto Rican pony we had at Newport.

When Kiffin was fourteen, his family went to live at Asheville, not a great distance from Newport, across the border of North Carolina. Asheville was at a higher altitude, a larger and more healthy city, with excellent schools. Kiffin attended the Asheville High School in 1906-1907-1908, but being intent upon a military career, entered the famous Virginia Military Institute, at Lexington, Virginia, in the fall of 1908.

He enjoyed the atmosphere of this great school, with its memories of Stonewall Jackson and other of America's most wonderful military chiefs, despite the strictness of the discipline and the severity of the hazing, which at that time was particularly bad. All the "rats," as the newcomers at the Institute were called, were beaten regularly and religiously with bed-slats, tin dippers, flats of bayonets, broomsticks, or anything that came to the hand of the masterful third-classmen.

I was at Washington and Lee University, whose campus was only a few hundred yards from the grounds of the Institute, and Kiffin came every Saturday for lunch at my fraternity house, and would often show me his stripes and bruises. I would fairly froth at the mouth with rage and indignation—I was never able to see him suffer, and even as a little boy would weep bitterly when Kiffin was punished for some mischief— but Kiffin would merely laugh in his dry way, and say that it was all in the game, and that the best way to make men of the "rats" was to haze them.

The summer of 1909, Kiffin received an appointment to the United States Naval Academy at Annapolis, having decided that there was more chance for action in the Navy than in the Army, and in the fall went up to Annapolis and entered "Bobby" Werntz' Preparatory School, to take a preliminary course for the Naval Academy entrance examinations. Here he met many other boys, also preparing to enter the Academy, and a number of Naval Cadets. Talking with these new acquaintances, he got the impression that it would be many a day before the United States Navy would see action, and caring nothing for naval or army life in time of peace, he wrote and asked me to try to influence our mother to let him resign his appointment and join me at Washington and Lee University.

Our mother readily consented, saying that she only wanted Kiffin to do that which would make him the most happy and the most useful in life, so about the end of November, 1909, he arrived at Lexington, and matriculated at Washington and Lee University. He was initiated into the Sigma Phi Epsilon fraternity, which counted amongst its members most of the men from Asheville, at Washington and Lee. By a sad coincidence, the only two other members of the Washington and Lee chapter of Sigma Phi Epsilon to fall in the Great War were also from Asheville, and had been intimate friends of Kiffin at the high school there: Lawrence Loughran, killed July 28, 1918, as a lieutenant-pilot attached to the Royal Flying Corps, and Fagg Malloy, cavalry-lieutenant, who died October 22, 1918, during the terrible influenza epidemic in France.

Kiffin's life at Washington and Lee was a very happy and carefree one. He was bright enough not to have to grind in order to learn his lessons, and had plenty of time to mix with the other students. A good judge of human nature, he did not quickly make friends with people and accept them into his intimacy; but he was never discourteous to anyone, and when he deemed someone worthy, he was a real and devoted friend. Therefore, he was very popular and well liked among his fellows. Tall and handsome, with clear blue eyes, a graceful dancer and of a pleasing manner, he was much sought after by the girls, but he was not of a sentimental nature, and was quite unspoiled.

Here again at Washington and Lee, Kiffin found everything to inspire his liking and desire for military life. General Washington had endowed the school, which before the Confederate War had been called Washington College; General Robert E. Lee had been president of the institution from shortly after the close of the war until his death, and was buried with other members of his family in the Lee Memorial Chapel. As was the case with the Virginia Military Institute, the graduates and students of Washington College had distinguished themselves upon the battlefield, and had left many lasting memories at Lexington, and General Lee seemed ever present there. Perhaps the only study in which Kiffin had a real interest was history.

As I look back, it is clear to me that Kiffin was all this while only unconsciously marking time. He was in school more from family habit and tradition than from a real desire to follow classical studies. He usually had a far-away, dreamy look in his eyes, and often seemed to be living in another world from that surrounding him.

In 1912, he decided to see something of the world, at least that part of it lying inside the boundaries of the United States and Canada. He made a trip to the Pacific Coast and then through Western Canada, thinking perhaps he might find a place where he would like to settle and make his home. Next he spent several months in San Francisco, which he liked greatly— after he came to France, he said that the life in San Francisco was more nearly like that of France than any other place he knew in America—and he came very near stopping there. At this period of his life, Kiffin liked to appear older than he really was, and never admitted that he was younger than at least twenty-five. He started in San Francisco an advertising agency, and had at one time working for him some twenty people, all of them considerably older than himself. Many of them probably would have been much humiliated had they known they were taking orders from a mere lad of nineteen years! He also thought of founding, in California, a paper or magazine.

But in spite of his youthful and impatient idea that the Southern people were old-fashioned and "set in their ways," the urge to come back home to the South was always strong within Kiffin. So in the fall of 1913, he returned to Asheville and spent a few months with his mother there. On New Year's Day of 1914, he joined me at Atlanta, Georgia, where I was then living. I shall never forget that morning when Kiffin arrived. I had been up late the evening before, properly ushering in the New Year, and was asleep at the Georgia Tech chapter house of our fraternity when I was awakened by the feeling that someone was watching me. I opened my eyes, and there stood Kiffin at the foot of my bed, with an amused expression on his face. I was amazed to see how tall he had grown; he was then a little over six feet two inches, having grown fully three inches since I had seen him.

We spent the day talking over anything and everything. I was full of curiosity as to his impression of the places he had seen, and Kiffin wanted to know if I really liked Atlanta well enough to make it my home. We agreed never again to part company, but to live together, and began making plans for leaving the fraternity house and finding a suitable bachelor's apartment.

Both of us rather liked writing. Our father, although only twenty-six years old when he died, had written and published in various magazines and papers a number of poems and essays very highly spoken of as showing considerable promise. We discussed starting some sort of magazine or publication, and did get out the following March a rather unsatisfactory paper called "The Commerce of Greater Atlanta," intended to boost our adopted city. Kiffin also achieved considerable success, considering the short while he was in Atlanta, with the Massengale Advertising Agency, the largest house of the kind in the South. He had decided that there was about as much romance in advertising as in any other settled-down, peace-time calling, and enrolled as a student of a course in modern advertising with some correspondence school. But this was not what his ardent nature really yearned for, and he was constantly restless.

We were in Asheville with our mother for a few weeks in June and early July. When we returned to Atlanta, the war clouds were already gathering over Europe. We had an apartment in West Peachtree Street, with a fairly efficient Negro boy as cook, butler, and general factotum. The last Sunday in July, we sat for a long time at the lunch table with two other Atlantans of about our age. Kiffin and I talked of the war which seemed inevitable, and of how interesting it would be to go over and fight for France. Both of us were fairly well read in French history, especially that of the "Ancien Régime" and of the Napoleonic Wars. We did not admire the French Revolution, and knew little of the history of the country during the nineteenth century, except the Franco-Prussian War, about which the stories of Guy de Maupassant and others had made our blood boil.

Our two friends, nice young Americans of good education, but small imagination outside their business, agreed mildly that it would be a great thing to fight against the Germans, and turned the conversation to the hands they had held in their last poker game.

After lunch, Kiffin called me aside and very seriously told me that he had been thinking a great deal during the past several days about the coming war, and that if I really wanted to go to France and join the French forces, his mind was fully made up to go. Talking together, our minds became more and more inflamed at the thought of what a general European war must be, and of the possibility of our country being drawn into it. Kiffin felt that it could not escape developing into a world war, and we then and there decided to offer our services to our favorite among the nations—France.

The following morning, Monday, we composed and mailed the following letter:

INTRODUCTION

136 W. Peachtree Street,
Atlanta, Georgia.
August 3, 1914.

HIS HONOR THE FRENCH CONSUL,
New Orleans, Louisiana.
DEAR SIR:

I desire to offer my services to the French Government in case of actual warfare between France and Germany, and wish to know whether I can report to you at New Orleans and go over with the French reservists who have been called out, or must I go to France before enlisting?

I am twenty-one years old, and have had military training at the Virginia Military Institute. I am very anxious to see military service, and had rather fight under the French flag than any other, as I greatly admire your nation.

If my services can be used by your country, I will bring my brother, who also desires to fight for the French flag.

Trusting to receive a favorable reply from you soon, I beg to remain

Yours most sincerely
KIFFIN YATES ROCKWELL.

Inquiries the next morning at the steamship ticket office in Atlanta brought the information that few steamers were leaving for Europe, that the British and French liners had put back into American ports, after being chased by German war vessels, and that it would be difficult to get abroad at that time. There was an American Line vessel, the *St. Paul,* sailing from New York on August 7th, however, and places might be had for us on board this boat, although it was sure to be crowded with people transferring from foreign ships.

We begged the steamship agent to telegraph to New York to see if berths could be had for us. A favorable reply was received on Wednesday, and, without waiting for a reply from the French Consul-General at New Orleans, we packed our belongings, leaving most of them behind, turned the apartment over to friends, and leaving faithful black Jim—who predicted that he would never see us again—in tears, we took the Thursday afternoon express for New

York.

When the *St. Paul* steamed out from New York harbor the following morning, we were aboard. Kiffin's letters which follow tell the story of the remainder of his life far better than anyone else could write it.

The clarity and simplicity of style of these letters is remarkable when the circumstances under which they were written are considered. Many were hastily scrawled with a pencil at odd moments snatched from Kiffin's duties in the trenches or in the air. Few were written under anything approaching normal conditions. They are given here without changes or corrections, though several to me were penned in moments of impatience or irritation, and express opinions or criticisms that Kiffin would have disavowed after calm reflection. Kiffin was not writing for publication, and he sometimes "let himself go."

It is well to give here, as an example of the impression he made on his war comrades, the chapter on Kiffin Yates Rockwell written by James Norman Hall, the celebrated writer and pilot of the Escadrille Lafayette, for the "Official History of the Lafayette Flying Corps":

KIFFIN YATES ROCKWELL

It is probable that Kiffin Rockwell was the first American to offer his services to France against the German aggressors, for on August 3, 1914, he wrote to the French Consul at New Orleans:

I desire to offer my services to the French Government in case of actual warfare between France and Germany, and wish to know whether I can report to you at New Orleans and go over with the French reservists ... or must I go to France before enlisting?

I am twenty-one years old and have had military training at the Virginia Military Institute. I am very anxious to see military service, and had rather fight under the French flag than any other, as I greatly admire your nation. If my services can be used by your country, I will bring my brother, who also desires to fight for the French flag.

Rockwell was a born soldier. Both his grandfathers, Captain

INTRODUCTION

Henry Rockwell of North Carolina, and Major Enoch Shaw Ayres, of South Carolina, were officers of the Confederate Army, and a more remote ancestor was a captain on General Washington's staff during the Revolution. His nature was made up of the simple virtues of a medieval warrior—pride amounting almost to sensitiveness, energy, determination, dauntless courage, and unbounded faith in the justice of his cause. Such men are rare and unmistakable when met; they stand a little aloof from the rest of the world and radiate a sense of great things—an atmosphere which shames the cynic and stills the voice of the doubter. It is not difficult to imagine the train of reasoning which led him to enlist: a great war was about to overwhelm Europe; France was preparing to defend her frontiers and ideals against an aggression which menaced all human liberty; one's course was clear—one must enlist to fight for France. And the flame of his idealism never for an instant flickered. Long afterward, when he had come to know all the squalor and disillusion of war, he wrote to his mother:

If I die, you will know that I die as every man should—in fighting for the right. I do not consider that I am fighting for France alone, but for the cause of humanity, the most noble of all causes.

In August, 1914, accompanied by his brother Paul, Rockwell crossed to France and enlisted in the Foreign Legion. From the beginning, his record of service was a splendid one—months of dreary trench life with the infantry did nothing to diminish his enthusiasm or fighting spirit. On May 9, 1915, when the Legion stormed La Targette, he was severely wounded in the thigh, and transferred to the Aviation after a long period of convalescence. In the autumn, Victor Chapman wrote from Avord:

I find a compatriot I am proud to own . . . called Rockwell. He got his transfer about a month ago from the legion. He was wounded on the 9th of May, like Kisling; in fact half of the Deuxième de Marche were wounded that day, not counting the killed and missing. He gives the best account I have heard. Having charged with the Third Battalion and being wounded in the leg in the last *bouck,* he crawled back across the entire field in the afternoon. At this moment I have mixed feelings of pride, envy, and sorrow, for he has just received a postal from a friend who has returned to the Régiment. They were given a banner and three days ago were up where the big advance took place. On account of their reputation and the general understanding that they were reserved for attack, the Régiment must have been in the very thick of it and has enormous losses. . . . Rockwell is chafing because he changed too soon. "There is nothing like it" (he says); "you float across the field, you drop, you rise again … the *sac,* the 325 extra rounds, the gun—have no weight."

On the Alsatian front (May 18, 1916), Kiffin Rockwell shot down the first enemy plane credited to the Escadrille Lafayette. The combat was characteristic of the man and his method of attack. He told of it in a letter to his brother Paul:

This morning I went out over the lines to make a little tour. I was somewhat the other side of our lines when my motor began to miss a bit and I turned back. Just as I started ... I saw a Boche machine about seven hundred meters under me and a little inside our lines. I reduced my motor and drove on him; he saw me at the same time and began to dive toward home. It was a machine with a pilot and a machine-gunner, carrying two rapid-fire guns, one facing the front, and one facing the rear, turning on a pivot so that it could be fired in any direction. The gunner immediately opened fire on me and my machine was hit, but I didn't pay any attention to that and kept going straight for him until I got within twenty-five or thirty meters of his machine. Then, just as I was afraid of running into him, I fired four shots, and swerved my machine to the right to avoid having a collision. ... I saw the gunner fall back dead on the pilot, his machine gun fall from its position and point straight up in the air, and the pilot fall to one side of the machine as if he too were done for. The machine fell off to one side—then dove vertically toward the ground with a lot of smoke coming from the rear. I circled around, and three or four minutes later saw smoke coming up from the ground, just behind the German trenches.

It was his first combat—the first time he had encountered an enemy machine in the air—the first time he had fired his gun at a German plane! And with four shots (afterwards verified by the squadron armorer) he killed both pilot and observer and sent the machine down in flames!

In discussing men, the French used a phrase describing admirably a keen and bitter fighter—*Il en veut, il fait la guerre.* Rockwell had come to France to fight; not to loaf, "swing the lead," or pose as a hero—and when he went over the lines it was *la guerre à l'outrance.* He shot down several Germans so far in their own lines that even the combats were invisible to friendly observers. On the Verdun front, in July, 1916, he took part in forty officially reported combats; in August he fought thirty-four aerial duels. Wounded in the face by an explosive bullet, he refused Captain Thénault's offer to send him to a hospital for treatment, and after twenty-four hours in Paris to reassure his brother, he hurried to the front to fight and fly again. His letters to Paul Rockwell give us glimpses of an extraordinary driving energy and determination:

I had thought beforehand that yesterday and to-day I would try my damnedest to kill one or two Germans for the boys [comrades in the Legion] who got it this time last year—but I had no luck. Am tired out now; have been out four different times to-day, all the time going up and down. Once I dropped straight down from four thousand meters to eighteen hundred meters on a Boche, but he got away. It tires one a lot—the change in heights and the maneuvering.

The day after Victor Chapman's death he wrote:

He and I had roomed together and flown together a great deal, and I had grown very fond of him. I am afraid it is going to rain to-morrow, but if not, Prince and I are going to fly about ten hours and will do our best to kill one or two Germans for Victor.

Rockwell's brief and splendid life was ended by the most glorious of deaths—struck down in the heat of combat, twelve thousand feet above the earth. Flying with Lufbery over the Vosges, on the 23rd of September, 1916, Rockwell became separated from his companion, and attacked a German two-seater well inside the French lines. In his daring and headlong fashion, he plunged straight at the enemy, paying no attention to a stream of bullets from the observer. He did not open fire until at such close quarters that watchers on the ground thought a collision inevitable—his gun stammered faintly, and the Nieuport turned its nose down, losing one wing as it hurtled toward the earth. A great wound, where an explosive bullet had passed through his chest at the base of the throat, must have caused instant death. His loss was an irreparable one to the Escadrille Lafayette—for he was a rare combat pilot, and his chivalrous and romantic example brought out the finest qualities of his companions. His funeral was worthy of his life and death. Fifty English pilots and eight hundred R. F. C. mechanics, a regiment of French Territorials, a battalion of Colonials, and hundreds of French pilots and mechanics, marched behind his bier. At the grave, Captain Thénault said: "When Rockwell was in the air, no German passed . . . and he was in the air most of the time. . . . The best and bravest of us all is no more."

Kiffin Yates Rockwell as a Student at Washington and
Lee University, 1911

CHAPTER I

> *Hotel Imperial,*
> *New York City,*
> *Thursday, Aug. 6, 1914.*

DEAR MAMMA:

Well, Paul and I are sailing on the American liner, *St. Paul*, to-morrow morning at 10 o'clock.

We would have gone by home to see you and explain things if there had been time. But we had to do some hurrying to catch this boat and it was practically our only safe chance. It is the only boat leaving here in two weeks time flying the U. S. flag and we did not want to wait two weeks.

I don't want you to worry or feel bad. You have always told me that you wanted me to live my life without interference and this opportunity is one that only comes once in a lifetime. I would not have come with Paul if I had not felt it was really a great opportunity.

We stopped off in Washington to-day and got our passports. We also carry letters of introduction to Hon. Walter Page, Ambassador to Great Britain, and to Stovall, Ambassador to Switzerland. He used to spend much time at Kenilworth Inn and you probably know him. We are due to arrive in Southampton and from there will go across to Paris.

You know I have always been a great dreamer and I just couldn't keep myself from this trip, for I felt the call of opportunity. You

1

have always said you had great faith in my future and now is the time for you to prove it, by not worrying about me. I will write you often, but of course the mails will be uncertain. You can write me in care of the U. S. Embassy in Paris.

My actions have often appeared as if I didn't care about you and the rest of the family, but it isn't that way. It is just that I must and will live my life as I think best even though I am often mistaken.

I am completely tired out and have many things to think about and can't write you a good letter to-night. My only anxiety is that you will worry too much and I ask you please not to do that.

Very much love,

KIFFIN.

U. S. M. S. St. Paul,
August 14, 1914.

DEAR MAMMA:

We are now in the Irish Channel and expect to arrive in Liverpool at six o'clock this evening. We do not go to Southampton as the English Channel is closed.

I have spent a week of absolute rest, thinking neither of the past nor the future. Paul and I both feel the best we have in years and I think I have gained at least two pounds. We have enjoyed the trip. There is certainly a cosmopolitan bunch on board. Here are a few of them: the Duchess of Marlborough; two or three Lords; several Ladies and a few Knights; several U. S. army officers, including two generals, Col. Samuel Reber, chief of the aviation department of the U. S. Army (whom Paul and I have grown to know well); Dr. Seaman, a famous U. S. army surgeon; Irvin S. Cobb, and Will Irwin. There is also one De Besa, who calls himself a Brazilian count and has been dabbling in Mexican politics for several years and was on President Madera's staff. He is a 33rd degree Mason, has traveled all over the world and speaks several languages. Everyone has him down as a faker, but he is certainly most interesting to talk to. Then there is a Hungarian officer in the Red Cross who wants to get back to his country. I suspect him of being a spy. He is of the better class and has lived in all the great cities of the world, speaks fluently five languages. There are French and English reservists and adventurers

2

of all description, and several war correspondents. So you can see we have had something to keep us entertained.

The first three days out were fine; since then it has been rough. Monday morning we sighted an iceberg and it became rather cold. Later in the day we ran into a storm which lasted for two days and at least two thirds of the people were seasick. Paul and I, however, are good sailors and did not feel the effects.

Wednesday, we passed a British warship which caused a little excitement at first.

Night before last we had a mock trial and Irvin Cobb was presiding judge. Last night, we had a concert given for the benefit of the widows and orphans of seamen.

Paul and I will probably spend to-night in Liverpool and go to London to-morrow, where we'd like to spend a week before going on to Paris.

I hope you will realize that this is best for us both and will not worry.

Love to you and Agnes,

KIFFIN.

London,
August 24, 1914.

DEAR MAMMA:

We are still in London but expect to leave to-morrow morning. We have been constantly on the go and have seen a great deal of the city. At first I thought it would be hard to find my way around the city but I don't believe I would ever get lost here now. We spent Saturday afternoon in the British Museum, which is the most wonderful thing we have seen.

Everything is very quiet here now. Most of the Americans have gotten away or, at least, they are not rushing around as excitedly as when we got here. The people are very calm and business continues as usual. This is a very popular war and everyone expects it to last a long while, but is willing to fight it out. The Irish have stopped their fuss and are coming to the defense of the flag. The militant suffragettes have stopped their "raising Cain" and the ones in prison have been released.

3

Paul and I have decided to go to Paris in the morning. We were around to the French Consulate this morning and had our papers fixed up. We will send you our address later. We are leaving our trunk here at 37 Torrington Square, as it would be so much trouble to take it with us. Our mail will be forwarded from here in case we find we are going to stay long.

Will write you again in a few days.

Love to all,

KIFFIN.

Kiffin Rockwell (facing camera) en route to the Front
September, 1914

CHAPTER II

Letters from the Foreign Legion

2*ème* *Régiment Étranger,*
1*ère* *Section, Dépôt de Rouen, France,*
Aug. 31, 1914

DEAR MAMMA:

Paul and I are here drilling with the American corps and about sixteen hundred other foreigners from every land. I think Paul wrote you about our joining. As it is very hard to get letters through and we are not allowed to write much about what we are doing, will only tell you that both of us are well and feeling fine. It is, of course, a little rough, but it will make men of us both.

We left Paris Friday morning and arrived here in the afternoon. Since then we have been living the army life, except that we have not yet our uniforms. The American branch is quite a mixture, but there are several fine fellows. Yale, Harvard, Michigan, Columbia, Cornell and several other schools are represented by graduates. There are two or three college professors and two lawyers. We drill about six hours a day and have three hours that we do what we please. The rest of the time is spent loafing around barracks and doing odd chores. The barracks is an old school building. We get to bed every night between eight and nine, lights out at nine, and get up at five in the morning. The food is good, wholesome and well cooked. We have a sleeping bag furnished and an army blanket, and straw to sleep on.

6

Everybody is congenial and good-humored, all trying to make the company a good one. We had from eleven in the morning till eight at night off yesterday and spent most of the time looking over the town, which is, in an historical way, the most interesting city in France. This is in Normandy and the people from this section were the ones who invaded England successfully. The most interesting thing to us yesterday was seeing the dungeon where Jeanne d'Arc was imprisoned before being burned at the stake. The tower was built in 1205. Then there is here a famous cathedral and numerous other old buildings.

This will be the last letter I shall write you for some time, as they don't like for us to write letters, and they read them all and don't send them if one talks too much. Everyone uses postcards and I will "follow suit" after this. We do not expect to be here much longer but guess mail will be forwarded from this address.

We both hope that you will not worry, as this is a great thing for us to do.

Much love
KIFFIN.

Post Card
2ème Étranger, Toulouse,
Sept. 7, 1914.

DEAR MAMMA:

Came here last week, fifty-five hours on a freight car, thirty-two men in each car. We are fixed more comfortably than at Rouen, are working hard and have very little spare time. It agrees with us. Paul and I are gaining strength and have a healthy look in our faces.

Love,
KIFFIN.

Post Card
Toulouse,
Sept. 17, 1914.

DEAR MAMMA:

Have been too busy and tired to write even a card. We get up at four A.M. and work as much as fourteen hours a day. We are now fully equipped and expect to leave here soon. Hope to write you a

The First appearance of the United States Flag over a body of American fighting men in the World War. The Star Spangled Banner of the American Volunteers in the Second Foreign Regiment. Taken at Toulouse, September 30, 1914. Copyrighted P.A.R. 1919

letter in a few days. Both of us are feeling well.

KIFFIN.

Toulouse, France,
Sept. 25, 1914.

DEAR MAMMA:

Paul and I have received only one letter from you since being here. It was a note written Sept. 4, and addressed to London, and begging us to come home. The thought of you has been the very thing that has worried me since my enlisting. I realize how you feel, and did before I enlisted, but I don't think you should worry or feel bad. I am of such a temperament that if I didn't do things that seem strange to you, I could never be satisfied, myself, or make a success of my life. You would not wish my life to be a failure in my own mind, even if by doing so I should live many years and be always with you. If I should be killed in this war I will at least die as a man should and would not consider myself a complete failure. I know you must think me selfish and inconsiderate of your feelings, but I am not. You expect great things of me and I want to do great things, and can see a great future before me. If I am killed in the attempt to attain that future, I have at least done my best; that is all any of us can do.

Since being here I have taken more interest in life than ever before. It has brought out new feelings and thoughts in me. I think if anything will make a man of me, it is this giving as a volunteer one's best for an ideal.

To-morrow we leave here and will have no address except *France.* There will probably be times when I shall be unable to write for weeks. But please don't worry. If anything should happen to either of us you would hear before a letter could reach you. The government has your address and several of our friends have it. We are only a few Americans and if anything should befall any of us the news would be sent immediately to the States.

We have been working very hard and my feet have bothered me a little from a forced march we took the other morning. It is going to be a life of hardships but I am willing to go through them, and actually enjoy them. The only worry is *you.* But I hope you will be

9

proud of me instead of worrying over me.

Lots of love for you and Agnes,

KIFFIN.

Camp de Mailly,
Aube, France,
Friday, Oct. 16, 1914

DEAR MAMMA:

Your letter of Sept. 20 reached us the first of the week and the one of the 28th came to-day, showing that the mail service is getting a little better. We are always glad to get mail as we hear very little of what is going on outside.

Paul said he wrote you this morning, so I guess he told you of our trip from Toulouse here.

We have been here two weeks now and I have wanted to write you before, but we are always either busy or tired out and the writing conveniences are poor. We are still working very hard, as France expects a long hard war and wants her men well trained so they can stand it. I feel well and I think I can stand the hardships. Of course there is the danger of the bullets, but, as I have already written you, I am willing to take my chance and will go through everything willingly, always doing my best.

The news we have heard since being here has been bad. Eventually, the Allies will win, but I fear it will take a long time. Things are quiet here but nearly every day we hear the heavy cannonade from the front. I don't expect we will be here much longer but that does not necessarily mean we will go to the front when we do leave.

Mr. R. L. Mock, of 36 Central Avenue, Atlanta, has the things Paul and I left there, or knows where they are.

I must get ready for drill. Please look at everything in the right way—that everything will turn out for the best.

Lots of love,

KIFFIN.

Nov. 14, 1914.

DEAR MAMMA:

I will write you a short letter, on the chance of its going through, to let you know that Paul and I are both well and safe. We are still -at the front, but have been most of the time in the reserve trenches and therefore in no danger. Of course, the hardships are severe but we are standing them well and the outlook is bright. We hope soon to get to some town and rest up for awhile.

The French Army pays only one cent a day and we are both "broke." We left the money we brought over locked up in our trunk, and we have no way of getting at it. When we do get into a town, we will need to buy a few things, so if you will send us some money regularly it will "come in handy." Send by International Money Order, and never send more than ten dollars in one letter.

We have received many letters from you, all of which we enjoyed. We get our mail even when in the trenches.

Love to all, and *don't worry.* We will come out o.k.

KIFFIN.

Address % The Regiment, France.

Dec. 1, 1914

DEAR MAMMA:

Since my letter of Nov. 14, I have spent twelve days in the trenches and rest of time at work in the rear. Go back to the trenches to-night. We are so safely entrenched that there is practically no danger at all. Our losses have been mostly through sickness, as conditions are bad in that respect. We are getting along fine. Hope you got my letter, asking for money-orders of not more than ten dollars at a time.

Much love,
KIFFIN.

Dec. 10, 1914.

DEAR MAMMA:

Have received letters from you as late as Nov. 20th. Am living in anticipation of the package, though I know my getting it is very uncertain. Do not go to much expense or trouble with packages,

11

but if you find they come through, and you send any more, you might put in something like a little jam, peanut butter, etc.—also a few American cigarettes. It is more the idea than the quantity that would make them so good. We are beginning to get a few packages from Americans in Paris. This morning, a package came out of which I got a pair of socks, some tobacco and some chocolate. The American bunch has dwindled, only fifteen of us left. The others are either reformed or sick in hospitals or have gotten easier jobs—only one wounded.

I have spent twenty-one out of the last twenty-four days in the trenches. At first I suffered some from cold, but the trenches are now fixed up for winter, and we can now have fire at night when the smoke won't show. I am in fine physical condition.

This takes my "Merry Xmas" and "Happy New Year" to you all.

With all my love,

KIFFIN.

Dec. 26, 1914.

DEAR MAMMA:

Just a few lines to let you know that I am well and thinking of you. This is the sixth day that we have been in a small village in the rear of the trenches. It was to be six days of rest, but each day, at 11 A.M., we have gone out with our guns and picks and shovels and dug trenches until 4 P.M.

The same was to be done yesterday, Xmas, but about ten of us slipped off to a farmhouse and drank coffee and talked all day. This morning we went to work at seven and worked till eleven and then with the others until 4 p.m. To-night, we go back to the trenches.

I suppose Paul has written you that he is out of it, but his condition is not serious. I haven't heard, but am hoping he was sent to Paris.

We had plenty of good things to eat for Xmas, some of them bought and some sent to us from Paris. About the best thing was a Virginia ham given us by an American doctor who is in the Legion. It had been sent to him. We had candy, nuts, jam, cheese, etc., and I even had an orange given me by an Englishman, from a package he received.

The weather has been fine for the last few days, cold but clear.

Much love,

KIFFIN.

Dec. 26, 1914.

DEAR PAUL:

Received your letter yesterday, also saw your article in the *Daily Mail,* which we all thought well written. This is the sixth day that we have been here in C——, supposedly for a rest, but every day we have gone out at eleven o'clock and dug trenches until four o'clock. Yesterday, they did the same, but about ten of us slipped off and spent the afternoon at a farmhouse, drinking coffee and rum. This morning we went to work at seven and quit at eleven. To-night, we go back to the trenches. I have had an awful cold for the past week and have felt perfectly rotten. Mail was so congested that few packages have arrived. Only two came for the Americans and we split the things up among ourselves (that is, among the ones who claim to be Americans). We have had plenty to eat, but I don't think anything has been distributed that you would need or care for. There are socks, gloves, helmets, mufflers and all kinds of woollen goods for everyone. But they are only lice-traps, and really not needed, so I don't bother to load myself down with any. I haven't received any package from Hilda; if it comes I will send it on to you if possible; otherwise, eat it myself. Some man in Paris sent a package of two mufflers, two pairs of socks and two helmets for you and me, but nothing else. We are all loaded down with such things, so they are worthless, but I will write to-day and thank him.

I have not been able to locate your "Rubaiyat." Casey said his girl gave the films to Prince. I have your Toulouse book. Bill Thaw left day before yesterday to join an aviation corps. The English expect to be transferred to the English Army soon; they took the names of all the English, and Rapier wanted to add my name. I had rather stay with France but sometimes I feel that this is a d—— rotten outfit, and I had best transfer, being handicapped by not speaking French. Send me a 2o-franc bill, to pay up my few debts. Dr. V——V—— [Van Voast] gave us a good Va. ham, which we all enjoyed very

13

much. As I said, we had plenty to eat for Xmas, but I didn't enjoy it much, owing to the bad cold. Hope you had a good Xmas.

Much love,

KIFFIN.

2ème Régiment Étranger,

Bon C. 1ère Cie.,

Dec. 29, 1914.

This is the third day back in the same trenches as we were in last. The line is a little more active. Last night our *petit poste* and a German patrol had a little scrap. They gave *"Aux armes."* We stayed out for a few minutes, then started back in, when the moon came out. It made the trees in the distance look like a vast wave of men coming across the field. Two or three officers yelled *"Aux armes,"* with their voices full of alarm, and there was much excitement for a few minutes. We were commanded not to fire until they were close, and then the mistake was discovered. Later in the night shrapnel shells burst right over us, and the Germans turned loose their machine-guns on the whole line of trenches. The fire was high, and no one was injured.

We have plenty of clothing and food, owing to packages arriving from Paris. Passed Rapier yesterday; he yelled "Hello! and live in hopes."

KIFFIN.

Jan. 7, 1915.

DEAR AGNES:

I have had practically no sleep for the last eighty hours, but I can't sleep now so will write you and try to keep my mind occupied.

I received your letter and the gold piece a few days after Xmas, in the trenches. I forwarded the letter to Paul but kept the money myself and thank you very much for it, and must say that you are very ingenious.

I spent the holidays fairly quietly, came out of the trenches New Year's Eve. New Year's Day we were marched ten kilometers to the rear and given the first bath the army had given us for three months. The next day we were inoculated for typhoid. The next two days our

14

arms were a little sore and we were more or less feverish; so we got two days' rest— the first since being in the army.

On the night of the 4th, almost midnight, we started to where I now am. This is a village that I should say probably had five thousand inhabitants before the war and it has been fought over quite a bit, the Germans having lost two thousand killed in a night attack on it in the early part of the war. There is now not a building that has not been demolished by shells.

The march here was through swamps and it was dark and rainy, so it took us about three hours to get here. We marched quietly through the streets and my section was sent to the sector nearest the enemy, which was a beautiful château (probably belonging to some millionaire) with a fine park all around it. When we got to it, we relieved the section there who had been staying in the basement, it being intact. While the relief was going on the ninth squad (the one I am in) was called off by the sergeant as *petit poste*. We went through the park about one hundred yards and came to a wall that was like the walls built around castles in medieval times. There were nine of us and our corporal (our number in camp was fifteen). Four of us were stationed at different points along the wall as sentries, while the others went down to the station for the *petit poste*.

At my position a shell had blown a hole through the wall. This hole had a door, propped up against it by a ladder, a small opening being left at each side, from which I could watch the direction of the enemy. Once in a while I would crawl up the ladder and look over the wall.

I was stationed there about four o'clock. At 7 o'clock, when it was getting light, the corporal came and told me to go back to the Château for food for us, which I did. There, I met one of the other guards and we got the food and started back with it. As we came out of the woods towards the wall we saw that we were exposed to fire from three directions and that the German trenches were quite near the wall. About that time bullets began to "whizz," and we "ducked" and ran to the wall and then along the side of it about two hundred yards to the *petit poste*. All that day we crouched in little dug-outs and cursed our officers for putting us in such a death-trap without more men and without telling us the real situation. At nightfall, we were stationed in such a way that four of us had to watch a wall practically one half mile long, right under the nose of the enemy, with hundreds of men in the rear of us subject to an attack. The *poste* was two hours on and two hours off, with no man to close his eyes, and the understanding that we would be relieved at six the next morning.

At ten-thirty P.M. I was standing at the door mentioned above when the communication sentinel came up to me. Just as he started to speak something fell at my feet and sputtered a little and then went out. We each said," What's that?" I reached down and picked it up, when the other sentinel said, "Good God! It's a hand-grenade!" I threw it away and we both jumped to attention, asked each other what to do, and finally decided for Seeger (the other sentry), to go to the *petit poste* for the corporal, while I watched. Just as he and the corporal came running up the corporal called *"Garde à vous, Rockwell,"* and another grenade fell at my feet. I jumped over the ladder toward the corporal and as I reached his side the bomb exploded. We both called out *"Aux armes."* We had no more than done this when the door gave in and a raiding band entered the side of the opening. The corporal and I both were in an open position at their mercy, so we turned and jumped toward cover. I went about ten feet when a rifle flashed and I dropped to the ground. When I dropped the corporal fell beside me and I knew by his fall that he was dead. I crouched and ran, the bullets whizzing by me, but I made it to the woods. In the meantime, the five men left at the *poste* jumped over to their positions. When they did the Germans in the trenches, at the door in the wall, and others who had managed to slip over the wall at some unprotected point, opened fire on them. Two were slightly wounded and another's rifle was shattered by a bullet. They immediately dropped flat on the ground and lay there, afraid to fire as most of the fire was coming from the direction in which they expected reinforcements, and in which they knew we sentries were. I lay in the woods and watched, not daring to move lest I be seen.

While they had us in this position, part kept firing while others ran down to the corporal, dragged his body up toward the door, cut off his equipment and coat and took them and his gun, broke his body up with the butts of their rifles and then got away without a shot being fired on our side.

A few minutes later a sergeant with two men came running through the woods, and Seeger (who had joined me) and I halted them and we five advanced on the opening and put up the door. By that time reinforcements came up.

Written four days later and sent in same letter

Corporal Weideman was a full-blooded German, but a naturalized Frenchman, having been in the Legion for fifteen years. He was ignorant but honest, impartial and afraid of nothing (something that can be said of few legionnaires). In my mind he was the best of all the old legionnaires.

The affair was rather a disgrace for all of us. I made mistakes in my actions due to not being well versed in all kinds of warfare. The corporal acted wrongly through ignorance and astonishment. The whole thing impressed all of us more like a murder than warfare. The Germans had no military point to gain by doing what they did. It was done as an act of individualism with a desire to kill. The top of poor Weideman's head was knocked off, after he was killed, by the butt of a rifle.

After the reinforcements came up they scattered in search of Germans while I resumed my post with the corporal's body beside me. In about fifteen minutes the Red Cross men came and got it and I called the acting chief of the squad and told him he would have to relieve me as my nerves had gone all to pieces. He did this and I went back to the château to make a report on how it all happened.

After about half an hour I came back to my post and was on guard practically all the rest of the night at another post.

About two hours after all this happened there came from the German trenches the most diabolical yell of derision I ever heard. It was mocking Weideman's last words, his call *"Aux armes,"* and it practically froze the blood to hear it. Up until that minute I had never felt a real desire to kill a German. Since then I have had nothing but murder in my heart, and now no matter what happens I am going through this war as long as I can.

At daybreak we were relieved and I went back to the château but couldn't sleep that day. At night we were relieved by another section and went to another château where I was out on *petit poste* again. The following morning I came in and felt that I must sleep. I lay down and was just getting to sleep when some excitable fool called a false alarm of "Aux *armes,*" and I could not get back to sleep. In the afternoon, I started writing to you, was sitting in the doorway, and got up to get more paper. When I came back German sharpshooters were firing at the position, so I had to give it up. That night I was on *petit poste* again, also the following night, until we were relieved early in the morning, and came back here, where I now am—about five kilometers to the rear.

Nothing could be worse than those four days and nights. The uncertainty of it all—lying in the rain and mud, eternally watching and listening, knowing that everywhere men were prowling, trying to slip up on one another in the dark and kill.

I have had my second inoculation for typhoid fever and am not feeling well to-day, but will be all right by to-morrow, I suppose. To-morrow night we will go back to some point on the line.

With much love,
KIFFIN.

Jan. 11, 1915.

DEAR PAUL:

Haven't heard from you for a long while; will not mail this letter until to-morrow, in hopes of having your address. If I don't hear, will send this, and forward other mail. Have been unable to write myself, owing to what I have been going through. There were six days and five nights that I practically didn't sleep. Four days and nights of it I was on *petit poste* at different sides of the town that our first trenches faced. The first night, I was on guard at a wall surrounding a château. We were right on the German trenches, and they were higher than we were, so had the advantage. At about ten-thirty o'clock, I was watching at a place along the wall where a shell had blown a hole through it. There was a door propped up by a ladder against it, leaving a small opening at the side out of which I watched, once in a while crawling up the ladder to look over. The *petit poste* was about fifty yards along the wall from me, on the other side it was about two hundred yards to the next sentinel. Seeger was the communication sentinel. It was a case of three men watching a

18

Kiffin Rockwell (left) on duty in Aisne Trenches
January, 1915

position, where there should have been twenty.

At about ten-thirty, Seeger had just come up to me, when something fell at my feet and sputtered a little, then went out. I picked it up. It was a hand grenade. Seeger ran for Corporal Weideman; as they came rushing back up, Weideman yelled, *"Garde à vous, Rockwell,"* and I heard something fall beside me. I jumped over the ladder towards the Corporal. As I reached his side, the grenade exploded. We both yelled, "Aux *armes."* At the same time the door came in, and we caught the flash of rifle fire. Seeger had jumped to the woods. Weideman and I were exposed and taken by surprise. We jumped towards cover, went about ten feet, and I saw the rifles flash again. I dropped to the ground; as I did so, Weideman fell beside me, and I knew by his fall that he was dead. I arose crouching and ran, three bullets whizzing by me before I reached the woods. When all this happened the five fellows at the *poste* jumped up on a platform by the wall. The Germans at the doorway, the Germans in the trenches and other Germans who had slipped over the wall at some unprotected point all opened fire on them. A bullet clipped "Cap's" ear, another went between Zinn's fingers, skinning each of them, another shattered Buchanan's rifle. They all fell off the platform and lay flat in the mud, afraid to fire for fear of hitting some of us.

I lay in the woods, covering the path to the *poste,* but afraid to move or be seen. My rifle had jammed, and I could not fire. While we were in this position the disgraceful thing to the Ninth Squad happened: without our firing a shot the Germans passed through the doorway, knocked the top of Weideman's head off with the butt of -*a.* rifle, took his gun, coat and equipment, and all got away.

Soon, Teresien came running through the woods with two men. Seeger had joined me, and we halted them; then we five advanced to the doorway and closed it up. The rest of that night and the next three days and night I spent on guard, and so did everyone except the ones out prowling in search of Germans. The whole town was demolished; everywhere were barricades and dead bodies. It was a hell of a time, and everyone's nerves were shattered when we came back here for a rest. I would like to write you a good description of it all but am not in condition to do so. Probably go back some place to-morrow night.

Love,
KIFFIN.

Jan. 15, 1915.

DEAR PAUL:

Haven't heard from you for a long while but hope you are in Paris. Just got back from eight days in the place where Weideman was killed. We were not allowed to send any mail and they are putting a strong censorship on all our letters; have threatened to cut off all our correspondence if we are not careful about what we write. Have written you all along, and forwarded a lot of mail. I have not received any packages, except the ones sent around Xmas for the Am. Vol., therefore have been short this month. We have had little chance to spend money. The English leave to-morrow, but I will not go with them; will stick it out in the Legion.

Love,
KIFFIN

Jan. 19, 1915.

DEAR PAUL:

Received your letter from Château-Thierry yesterday, first I had heard for a long while. I wrote one letter and one card to Montmirail, telling what I had been doing and of Weideman's death. I have just got back this morning from another four days in the village death-trap; had about five hours sleep during the four days, being on *petit poste* every night. Night before last I crouched by the wall for fourteen hours in the sleet and snow, with my gun loaded and the magazine open. There were four of us and a corporal, with orders that if we moved from the posts, no matter what happened, we would be courtmartialed. We got away all right, but this morning about fifteen minutes after the *poste* I was on was relieved by Bon D. they got shot up; don't know how many were killed.

I have been well ever since you left, perfect health, have gotten strong and hardy and stood it better than anyone, but the mental and physical strain we have been under this month is breaking us all down. It has been worse than if we had been having big battles. I have experienced more and done more work and guard than anyone else in the section and it is telling on me now. That terrible guard night before last was with the first section, only three men from the third section, because the first was short three men for the different posts. The others of the third had a rest.

There are all kinds of rumors to-day. You have probably heard bad news about the line a little way north of here. Well, we know we are going to change in the next day or so. We don't know whether it means the rear for a rest, or whether it means real hard action. Anyway, we move. I may get to some place where money will be useful, and I want to take a bath and clean up generally, as soon as I get a chance. So you might send me some money; it wouldn't be a bad idea to wire it, as the Bureau Central would forward, regardless of where I am. I suppose you have gotten in touch with the account mamma has started for us in England.

I don't know about the English Volunteers. Rapier has left. If you can get me into a French regiment, get busy, for I want to get out of the Legion. This regiment is no good; the officers are no good. It is just luck I am not dead, owing to their d——d ignorance and neglect. The only thing in their favor is that they have fed us well lately. They brought hot tea to us at midnight last night on guard; rations have been increased all around.

I am going to sleep now.

KIFFIN.

Jan. 21, 1915.

DEAR PAUL:

I have written you letters to both Montmirail and Château-Thierry, also forwarded a bunch of letters, because I felt you were more sure to receive them that way than by my keeping them, as our life is very uncertain these days. I have received a card from Nilson saying he was waiting to hear from you in order to forward mail. I think several of the letters I forwarded were important, so be sure to write for them at once. I wrote you, asking you to send me some money at once, as I think we are moving soon. I also wrote you that if you could get me transferred to a regular French regiment, to get busy at once. In regard to your coming back to this regiment, I will say for the last time, don't be a fool. At least one third of the men who left Camp de Mailly have gotten out of the Régiment , and elsewhere in the French service, and there are not five here but would change if they could. If you try hard and get sent back you will be no good inside a month; you will suffer a lot and finally reach the point where they will have to send you away. I know what I am talking about. I told the boys you were trying to come back and not a one of them but said that they thought you had more sense.

Love,
KIFFIN.

2ème Régiment Étranger,
Jan. 31, 1915.

DEAR MAMMA:

I suppose you are a little worried about me, owing to recent happenings, but have spent eight days in a position where we couldn't send any mail. They have put a strong censorship on all our mail and threaten dire punishment if we write too much. I am well and strong. We gave the Germans a nice birthday present all around where I was, but I didn't fire my rifle, although I came awfully close to having to do so. Our artillery, however, did splendid work.

I have never received your package. The parcels post was opened to the Allied countries the last of November and other fellows have received packages. Don't understand what is wrong with our P. O. However, I am getting along fine but would like for you to send me a two dollar Ingersoll watch in some way or other, but don't bother about other things. Don't worry about my welfare, for the more I see the more I am convinced that I am coming through safe and whole.

Winter will soon be over and I am glad of it, as the recent cold has made it a little hard. Am getting real fat from the outdoor life.

Love,
KIFFIN.

Feb. 1, 1915.

DEAR PAUL:

Received your letter this morning, was certainly glad to hear from you, also to receive the twenty francs. There is a farm here that is stocked up with chocolate, cheese, etc., and all of us have been feeding up, so you can see the money was greatly appreciated. The English left this morning. I was given the option of going or staying, and it may have been I am foolish, but I stayed. I figured that I came over to join with France and had stuck it out five months, so might as well continue. If you can get me into a regular regiment, that will be fine. The reason I keep writing you not to come back here is because I know that you are not able to stand it, and then there is no romance or anything to the infantry. It is not a question of bravery, it is a question of being a good day laborer. So if you don't want to leave the service, get into something that requires education and not brute strength. I personally am stronger than I have ever been in my life, but without one exception I am the only one. "Cap," Krogh, and all the fellows we thought strong have gone backward and been sick a lot. Out of the eighteen men of the Ninth Squad, there are only six of us in it now: myself, "Cap," Seeger, Dowd, Krogh and Nilson, who returned yesterday but who we all know will not be able to stick more than three or four weeks, owing to his stomach. Zinn has been put in the Mitrailleuses.

As far as fighting goes, we are always in danger of our lives but don't get a chance to protect ourselves, as this is mostly an artillery war. Of course, the infantry sometimes does fierce fighting, but seldom, and I believe it possible to go through the war without ever taking part in the kind of fighting we imagined we would do. You take a few days ago: a battle was raging on every side of us, and we were in a very advanced position. Our artillery near us did the most damage of any. It simply raked the valley, yet we didn't fire a shot. We sat with our rifles in our hands underground, ready to go out any minute and fight, but that was all. Well, I must go to work, so will close.

Love,

KIFFIN.

Young Towle left with the English, a good riddance.

Feb. 8, 1915.

DEAR MAMMA:

Little to write, just the same old life. Came back last night from four days at one of our most advanced positions here. The English in the Legion left for the English Army about a week ago. I could have gone but decided at the last minute that from a sentimental standpoint I would stick it out here even though it would be easier for me and my opportunities greater in the English Army.

I understand the relations between England and the U. S. are rather strained, but I hope there will be no trouble.

Our company was a rather dilapidated bunch that went to the front last time. What with the English gone and our losses in the last three and a half months in killed, wounded, sick and those transferred, we had only about a third of a company and part of those were men who came after we reached the front. The Ninth Squad has been the best known all along, for many reasons. When we left camp we were eighteen strong. When we went up last time there were only six of us and without a corporal, one of us acting as chief of the squad.

When we lost our old corporal we lost one of the greatest characters in the Legion. We often compared him to an eagle with the squad as his young. We later got a corporal who was the exact opposite in every respect. We thought of a sparrow instead of an eagle. He was a faker, lazy, a coward and a crook. He did not last long, however, before he became "sick" and was evacuated. They say it was the Ninth Squad that made him sick.

The work lately has been harder than ever, as we have been doing the work of a full company, but new men arrived from the depot to-day and we expect easier times. About half an hour ago the Ninth Squad received its allotment of six husky Alsatian rookies. We are already planning how we can let them do most of the work and take a little rest ourselves. To-day, we feel more like real soldiers than ever. We no longer grumble or kick, as we have found it does no good. We do everything now with an "I don't care" spirit and one of the main qualifications of a good soldier is *not to care.*

We have had beautiful weather lately and that has put me in a rather good humor.

25

Heard from Paul a few days ago. He seemed to be in pretty good spirits but keeps talking of coming back, which would be foolish. Have also had a letter from Irma, which I greatly enjoyed.

Much love,

KIFFIN.

2ème Régiment Étranger,

Bon C. 1ère Cie,

Feb. 16, 1915.

DEAR PAUL:

I would have written you earlier but I have been either too busy, too disgusted, or too uncomfortable.

The last four days we have been at a reserve post, the first since you left, and they were four miserable days. It rained or snowed the whole time. We worked three hours in the morning, four in the afternoon, and three each night; and our trenches were leaking water from the top, and water was seeping in at the bottom.

Nilson said that Hadley was still in the hospital. As you say, Nilson is a good lad, but he is a nuisance here and we do not expect him to last long.

I have just found out that the *vaguemestre* here has forwarded quite a bunch of our mail to the depot at Orleans, also whatever packages had come for us.

The Americans here now are Capdeville, Zinn, Dowd, Seeger, Trinkard, King, Phelizot and Chatkoff. Morlae is also here. He just came back, after studying a few weeks in a corporal's school. He is now the sergeant in charge of this section and a bigger —— than ever. He takes every opportunity to insult the Americans in front of superior officers, so as to try and curry favor with them. He and I are always at swords' points and I have told him that some day we will both be back in America. The first thing I shall do when we are back there is to beat hell out of him. None of us has any use for him. But you know how it is in the French army. A sergeant has it over a private. I have even been thinking of changing my company because I might really lose my temper some time and kill the blackguard, and you know what that would mean for me. I want you to keep this letter in regard to Morlae and if by any chance I do not get back to the United States, and he tries to get a lot of cheap notoriety over there, like he is after, this is what the Americans think of him.

The new corporal of the Ninth Squad is a Boer, who fought through the Boer War and lost his father, brothers and sisters in it. He has been in the Legion for ten years, and his time is up March ist. Then he will probably go back to his own country and fight against England. He is a soldier and a gentleman, and would probably be a captain now if he had his just deserts. *Just what* are the chances of another regiment for me; if not a regular French Régiment, the First Étranger?

With love,

KIFFIN.

To the Vicomte du Peloux
2ème Régiment Étranger,
Bon C. 1ère Cie.,
3ème Son.,
Feb. 16, 1915.

DEAR SIR:

I received your letter four days ago, for which I thank you very much.

I am well and getting along fine and have no right to complain of anything. I came back last night for repose, after four days at the front. They were uneventful, but a little uncomfortable, owing to the snow and rain.

In regard to my wants—I have been very lucky throughout the winter in having plenty of all necessities. However, I should like for you to send me some of the little luxuries we cannot get here at the front. I should also appreciate it very much if you could send me an English and French grammar, as my small knowledge of the French language has proved quite a handicap to me at times. What I desire is a beginner's grammar; in other words, one used by first-year students. I have very little spare time, but think I can find enough to do some studying.

We all look forward to the coming of spring, when we hope to advance and bring France victory.

27

Again thanking you and your wife for your interest in me,

Sincerely yours,

KIFFIN Y. ROCKWELL.

Feb. 28, 1915.

DEAR PAUL:

Received your letter yesterday, got the fifty francs; the package announced hasn't arrived yet. Spent six days on *petit poste* in an open trench close enough to hear the Germans talking. On guard all night. In the daytime, would slip down through the communication trench about one hundred yards and sleep in a covered trench. There were only twelve of us there but nothing happened except a little sharpshooting. Seeger had a bullet through his *capote* but it didn't break the skin. Zinn was evacuated yesterday. We had been trying to get him out for the last two or three months. He was a nice lad but a nuisance as a soldier. He was sick most of the time and would fall to sleep on guard and snore loud as hell. They gave him prison sentences and work but finally became convinced that he was really sick so now have sent him back. We have been busy cleaning up as we are going to be inspected by the General. It means a hike of fifteen kilometers to the rear and the exercising, then fifteen kilometers back here. Not pleasant to look forward to. We may go this afternoon.

That's all the news.

Love,

KIFFIN.

To the Vicomtesse du Peloux
2ème Régiment Étranger,
March 7, 1915.

MY DEAR MADAME:

I received your letter and appreciate it very much. The package has not yet arrived but suppose it will be waiting for me when I go back from the trenches this time. The time it takes for packages to come is very uncertain. I am looking forward to its arrival both for the grammar and for the "berries of life," as the latter have grown to be a great item in the life here at the front—not that the government fails to give us plenty, but I'll enjoy a change.

When we went back from the trenches last time we were told that we would probably march fifteen kilometers to the rear and be reviewed by General Joffre. It pleased us very much and we busied ourselves cleaning up and getting everything *règlementaire,* but the review did not take place. We were rather disappointed, for we wished to see General Joffre, and then there was a current rumor that it meant a change of sectors for us. You see, I left camp Oct. 19th, and came to this sector and entered the trenches on Oct. 27th. The trench I am now in is about seven hundred meters from the first trench I was ever in. I have made every trip to the trenches with my company except one, which was due to my feet being in very bad condition from the march here. Our record for length of time in the trenches is twenty-four days out of thirty. However, now we do not have it so hard, but spend half the time in the front and half in the rear. Our positions at the front are usually *petits postes* where there is no danger at all from artillery fire, and that is about all we have here now. Once in a while, we suffer from it when we are in the rear. If the enemy should take a general offensive in this sector, he would hardly attack our trenches but would probably try to push through on either side which, if successful, would mean our being cut off and surrounded. If we should take the offensive the line would have to be pushed back on each side of us before we move. So ail we can look forward to is staying here for quite a while yet, unless we get a change of sectors.

I don't care about a rest, for I am in fine condition and content to stay at the front until the war is over. But I have always been a great roamer and to have to stay in the same place is my greatest trial. So I keep hoping for the change in sectors. We have been very lucky; we have always had plenty to eat and to wear and have really not suffered any at all. We volunteers feel at times that we are only an expense to France instead of an aid to her. However, when we get the chance we will try to do our share.

Yesterday, I received letters from my mother and brother, both saying they had heard from you. It pleases my mother very much to know that you and your husband are interested in my brother and me, and it pleases us to know that you send her cheerful messages.

She is inclined to worry too much about us, but I suppose that is the way with all mothers. I am inclined to be a fatalist and don't see the necessity of her worrying as much as she does.

I hear the call *soupe* at the end of the trench and must close.

In answer to Monsieur du Peloux's card, my sector postal number is 6.

Assuring you both of my appreciation,

I am,

Sincerely yours,
KIFFIN Y. ROCKWELL.

Post Card

2ème Étranger,
March 11, 1915.

Received your letter the other day. I might as well stay where I am; get along pretty well, although local conditions are bad. The third section has been having trouble with the Mitrailleuse section, and we are practically under arrest now. That is, we can't go out in the streets because it would mean a war. Phelizot died night before last as the result of foul play in a scrap between him and two Arabs of the M. section, which afterwards turned into a battle royal between the two sections. However, don't mention this to anyone. Will write further particulars some other time. Received a nice package from the Vicomtesse du Peloux this morning. Good things to eat and a French grammar.

Love,
KIFFIN.

To the Vicomte du Peloux
1er Régiment Étranger,
Bon B. 2ème Cie., 4ème Son.,
March 18, 1915.

DEAR SIR:

I am changed to the *1er* Étranger. I wrote my brother some time ago that I would like to change from the *2ème* Étrg., if possible, to a regular French regiment. He found that impossible so had me transferred here. I can tell that this is a much better regiment and I am with five fine Americans, so am glad of the change. Have been here two days and am now in the trenches. I do not know where my brother is now. If you know, write him my address, please.

Sincerely yours,

K. Y. ROCKWELL.

Via Bureau Central Militaire, Paris,

1ᵉʳ Régiment Étranger,

March 21, 1915.

DEAR MAMMA:

I guess you will be surprised to see my new address. I wrote to Paul the early part of the year telling him I was dissatisfied with local conditions in the other regiment and asking him to see if it were possible for me to get into another regiment or into a regular French regiment. We found that owing to the laws of the country it was impossible for me to get into a regular French regiment and I was making up my mind to be contented where I was.

About a week ago I came in from working on trenches and was told I had been transferred to the *1ᵉʳ* Régiment and was to leave in two hours. I packed my sack in a hurry and rode that night with the first wagon to a town in the rear. The following morning I went to the headquarters of the Army Corps where the General and several other officers talked with me and treated me very courteously. I stayed there until six that evening, when I got into a limousine with a captain who spoke a little English and who took much interest in the fact that I came over to France for the war. I rode with him to the headquarters of another Army Corps where I spent the night. The following morning I climbed into a limousine with another captain who spoke perfect English and had been in the States. On our journey we came right through Rheims which was in a terrible condition from the continuous bombardment. This captain described to me all the surrounding country and gave me a number of interesting points on the war. The previous afternoon he had run the gauntlet, as you might say, having thirty shells burst around him before he could cover one hundred yards in his machine. A little beyond Rheims he stopped and I took a third automobile to my destination where I joined this outfit and came to the trenches with them that night. The change has done me worlds of good. My trip here was the most

31

pleasant thing I have experienced since leaving the States. When I got here it was a change of territory and a better regiment than the one I was in and better local conditions. I found five other Americans here in the Régiment who are a better lot than the Americans in my old company. One of them was at V. M. I. the year after I was. I am well pleased with everything.

To-day is the first day of spring and the weather testifies to it. I am sitting in the sun on the side of the trench writing this.

Much love,

KIFFIN.

To the Vicomte du Peloux

1er Étranger,

March 29, 1915.

MY DEAR SIR:

Received your card yesterday and was glad to hear from you and to learn that Paul was on his way to Paris.

Have been in first and second line trenches for thirteen days now and will probably stay nine or ten days longer. The lines are very close together here but we have exceptionally good trenches, so it wasn't very bad. A cheap watch would be very handy for me.

Regards to your wife.

Sincerely yours,

KIFFIN Y. ROCKWELL.

Post Card

1er Étranger,

April 1st, 1915.

DEAR PAUL:

Received your letter a couple of days ago, glad to hear from you and that you were in Paris. I have been in the trenches for sixteen days now and will probably stay a week longer, then go back for a week's repose. This is a better regiment than the Second was. More discipline, etc., but better soldiers and men you would have confidence in in case of action. There are five other Americans and not a bad bunch.

Love,

KIFFIN.

LETTERS FROM THE FOREIGN LEGION

1er Régiment Étrg.,
2ème Rég, de Marche,
Bon B. 2ème Cie., 4ème Son.,
Secteur Postal 109,
April 10, 1915.

DEAR PAUL:

I have been intending to write you a letter for a long while but haven't felt like writing any at all lately. When I received notice of being transferred, I had just come in from work and it was about 4:30 o'clock. They told me I was changed to the 1er Étranger and was to leave at 6:30. It was a surprise to me and a rush order. I left some of my things there, washing, for instance. However, I had little regrets at leaving the outfit, although things were at the best stage for me that they had ever been in. Capdeville and I were practically running the 9th, and Morlae had suddenly become exceptionally friendly towards me, owing to my having "got his number" on a few things. Our Lieutenant, who had always been very friendly to me, had just been made captain of the company.

But I came here and found conditions very good: good officers and the men are good soldiers, an entirely different outfit from the 2ème. We went to the trenches the night I arrived here and stayed for twenty-two days in them, and then came here for a week's rest two nights ago. Things were rather quiet in the trenches. The lines are very close together in a field that is level as a floor. The trenches are laid out so that it is almost like an underground city. The Regt. made them this winter. They are about eight feet deep and three feet wide and wind around in every direction so that you can walk for hours, all of them leading into the front combat trench, which is especially well made, having loopholes every two feet and a little place to stand in when shooting. I think that nearly the whole Division Marocain is in that field with us. The Zouaves were about one hundred meters from us. They have an exceptionally good reputation for fighting.

There are five Americans with me, not a bad lot; four of them, however, cannot speak French as well as I. The Sergeant is a very nice fellow but we lose him, as he has been named sous-lieut. The man who takes his place as sergeant is the former corporal of the 13th Squad. He is an old Legionnaire, but has been very attentive to the

Americans. He squandered seventeen francs last night on a dinner for me and the one American who speaks French. But he is doing it with the idea that we will spend a lot of money on him. But I have worked awfully hard for over seven months and have gone through a good many hardships; I am tired out now and am bothered very much with rheumatism, so if I can make my life a little easier by bribing my sous-officers with food, etc., I will not hesitate to do so. So far, since being here, I have had it pretty easy. I am running out of clothes and would have written the Vicomte du Peloux for some, but hate to put him to so much trouble, so thought I would write you about it. I have forgotten what we left at the hotel, but if there are two or three two-piece suits of underwear there, send them to me. If there are not any there, buy me three suits of light weight, the size that you wear, also two pairs of heavy socks.

I am looking forward to receiving the box of "eats" announced. I have written to the other regiment for my mail, but all I have received is one card from you, one from mamma, and two that I enclose. Perhaps part of the mail was returned to the depot at Orleans; in that case I suppose it will be sent to you. The packages Mrs. Coumbe writes about will probably be lost or eaten by someone else.

I hope you are feeling well by now but not to see you back in the trenches.

The weather is cold to-day.

Love,
KIFFIN.

1er Régt. Étranger, B. 2,
April 17, 1915.

DEAR PAUL:

I was very glad to receive your letter this afternoon as it was all I had heard from you for over a month, except one card. I have written the other Regiment and two of the fellows about my mail, but all I have received is what I wrote you of. I have been hoping to hear that you are going to be discharged, for I know you are not physically able to come back to the trenches and stand the life.

I received the underwear at the same time as the letter. I was glad they were not warm suits, but would have preferred something

34

in the line of B. V. D.'s as they are easier washed, and easier for clearing of lice, but this is good underwear, so am satisfied.

In regard to seeing a doctor and getting evacuated, I have never reported at sick call once since you left. I may be wrong, for I still have very painful rheumatism in my arms and hands, but I have been conscientious about doing my best ever since I enlisted.

At first I was handicapped very much by not knowing any French. Now, however, I speak a little and understand more. They all treat me now as being a good soldier. The corporal shows a little favoritism towards me; more than to anyone else in the squad. The sergeant asked me not long ago if I wanted to be a candidate for corporal. That, however, meant drilling when the others were at rest; and then, the men do not like the ones who get to be corporal that way, so I said "No." However, I really feel that if I could speak French a little better I would make a better officer than many of them here. Being in the war is probably the only useful thing that I have ever done or ever will do, so while I am in it I want always to do my best; and if I am killed in it, I will be perfectly contented to die, more so now that you are getting all right, and I know that you will prove to mamma that her sacrifices and worrying have not been wasted. Even if I come out of the war, I am afraid that that will be up to you, for I have lost my ambition for what the world calls success.

I do not want to go to the doctor and be evacuated, although there are very few who have been in the trenches as long as I and not gone back for a rest. If, through any other means, I am given a rest, I will be glad to accept it.

As regards a commission as sous-lieutenant, I doubt if that will be possible. However, I may get a chance to show my ability, and merit a commission.

About the Americans here, one is Kenneth Weeks, an author of several books who has lived in France for several years with his mother; another is Russell Kelly, who went to the Virginia Military Institute in 1910, the son of a lawyer in New York City; another is John Smith, an adventurer, who served in the Spanish-American War, was a sergeant in the Philippines, has lived in the Orient, in Alaska, and many other places; another is Laurence Scanlon, a New

York electrical engineer, and young. These three men came over in November on horse boats. The last is "Skipper Pavelka," sailor and wanderer, has never had any ambition, otherwise could probably have made a success as he has quite a lot of genius in several ways. Weeks has plenty of money and speaks perfect French. The other four have no money and do not speak French as well as I. Weeks and I share what we have with them and the six of us stick together pretty close and get a lot of pleasure out of being together. Weeks is now cooking chocolate and we are going to eat some of the cake with it that arrived in the package you and the Vicomte and Vicomtesse du Peloux packed, and which I am enjoying greatly.

I have been back in the trenches for three days now, and probably will be here about three weeks longer. This trench is a little to the rear of the first line trench where we go to-morrow. This whole field is nothing but a network of trenches. The town I was at for *repos* is where we rested four days last fall. It has more civilians now than then, and when we were there this time we could buy anything to eat that we wanted. The Germans shell it almost every day, and there have been a number of women and children killed there.

I am able to get matches now and do not need a briquet. If you could get a Rubaiyat in Paris and send it to me, I would enjoy reading it.

Give my regards to the Vicomte and Vicomtesse du Peloux, tell them that I received the package of "eats" and thank them, and that I will write soon.

Much love,
KIFFIN.

P. S. Seeger was alive when I left the Second Régiment. Phelizot got in a scrap with two drunken Arabs of the Machine Gun Section, and a third Arab slipped up behind him and hit him on the head with a two-liter *bidon* full of wine. The wound was neglected, and Phelizot was not excused from service when he said he was seriously hurt. The next day, he fell by the roadside, where a lieutenant found him paralyzed and lockjaw setting in. He died two days later, after horrible suffering. The only time he could speak was just before he died, when he raised up out of bed, and pulled the American flag from around his waist, and cried, "I am an American."

Phelizot had given quite a lot of money to the war sufferers, and had nine thousand francs on him when he died.

To tine Vicomte du Peloux

1ᵉʳ Étranger,
Apr. 21, 1915.

DEAR SIR:

I have only time for a short letter as that long-looked-for period of repose has arrived. We leave the trenches to-night for the rear and for a rest. I do not know where we will go. The depot is at Lyon and we may go there or we may be sent to Camp Mailly.

I am enclosing an international money order for ten dollars that one of the boys here has and does not know how to get the money. His name is Russell Kelly, who went to Virginia Military Inst. the year after I was there. The sender is James E. Kelly, his father, a lawyer, whose address is 45 Broadway, New York City. This is the first money Kelly has had since being here, so I would like for you to send it to me at once and charge to my account until order has been cashed. Also, send me one hundred francs, as I may need it in repose. If we are in the rear long I will try to get to Paris, though I have no idea what the chances are.

I received your letter yesterday and enjoyed hearing. I really had plenty of clothes all winter, and the reason I wrote Paul about the underwear was for summer. I consider that I have put you to enough trouble without having you do things that Paul can do for me. I received the package of eatables the second day, back in the trenches, and have enjoyed all the contents. I was glad it came while I was in the trenches.

Tell Paul about my being on the way to the rear.

Regards to your wife.

Sincerely yours,
KIFFIN Y. ROCKWELL.

P. S. Address me the same as before.

Apr. 22.

I will leave my letter the same, but we did not leave last night. We got everything ready and expected to go and did leave the trenches we were in but stopped in others more in the rear. They say this stop is only temporary and that we will leave any time now within the next two or three days. Of course something may happen to prevent, but I really think we are going this time.

The captain had a telephone message last night, saying Italy had declared war on Austria. Most of our Company are Italians so it created great excitement. Haven't heard the message confirmed, but hope it is true.

K. Y. R.

To the Vicomte du Peloux

1er Étranger,
April 28, 1915.

DEAR SIR:

We started to Lyon for repose, at least all the officers and everyone thought so. But orders were evidently changed while we were en route, for we are now in the rear of the lines getting a little rest after a very strenuous trip—very heavy firing in front of us. We went through Paris about midnight of the a6th but the train did not stop ten minutes, as we were then making fast time and turned north from there. I was disappointed but after eight months one gets indifferent.

Note address on other side of card.

Sincerely yours,
KIFFIN Y. ROCKWELL.

To the Vicomte du Peloux

1er Étranger,
May 2, 1915.

DEAR SIR:

I received your two letters yesterday with the *mandat* for 151.50 francs and am returning the money order, signed by Kelly. Haven't been to the trenches yet since coming up here. In fact I am very puzzled as to what we are up to, as we keep moving around. We are now within one kilometer of a railroad station and it would not surprise me if we take train again for some other sector, though we may go straight into the trenches from here. We get the papers, and of course they explain a good deal to us. Anyway, whatever we are planning to do, it is a great change from the last six months and to me is proving a mental and a physical rest.

We have had a number of rumors regarding Italy and other countries but I am of the same opinion as you and will not believe Italy in the struggle until I see it. I think Italy has shown herself a coward and very selfish, but in spite of that the Italians in the Legion have proved themselves very good soldiers and I like the ones we have in this company very much.

It is fine weather here and we are all taking life about as easy as possible in the army.

Tell Paul about this letter.

Regards to your wife.

Sincerely yours,
KIFFIN Y. ROCKWELL.

May 2, 1915.

DEAR MAMMA:

I left the trenches at midnight of the 24th ult. Since then we have been doing quite a bit of traveling. When we left we thought we were going to Lyon for repose and then go to the Dardanelles, but when we passed through Paris at midnight of the 26th, and turned north, we knew that was all off. We have been in the rear of the lines at different places now for several days and expecting to go into hard action at any time; we are now back within a half mile of a railroad station, and for all we know we may embark for some other sector.

The weather has been very hot, but what marching we have done has been short stretches at a time and I have really enjoyed it all. It has been such a change from the last six months and has been interesting to see the country and also the large movements of troops, artillery, many aëroplanes, Zeppelins, captive balloons, etc. There is quite a change in the civilians also. They are not so hysterical and excitable, and instead of crying, they give one a cheerful smile.

Paul wrote me that the Atlanta papers had been giving me quite a lot of publicity and that the *Journal* had published my letter to Agnes. Others also have written me, and all of you write and act as if you thought I came over here for notoriety and to try to be a hero. It has hurt me and made me mad also to think how few people there are who give me credit for any strength of character. Maybe the restless life I have led justifies all in their opinions. However, I am sorry that such is the case and it means to me that I will never try to live in the South.

I just had my beard cut off to-day and shaved for the first time since being in the army. I had a fine beard but it made me look very old, at least fifteen years older than without it, they all say.

Well, the *soupe* is here, so will eat.

Lovingly,

KIFFIN.

1er Étranger,
Bon B. 2ème Cie.,
May 5, 1915.

DEAR PAUL:

Would have written you sooner but have not done any writing to speak of lately. I suppose the Vicomte du Peloux told you that we had changed sectors. Since the 24th of last month I have not done much of anything but travel around and at the same time have as good a time as possible. The last four days we have all been eating and drinking to a fare-you-well. We have been able to get all the wine we wanted, and things to make special meals. Each day we have had a big party. The only time we have done any work was night before last when we went to the trenches ten kilometers from here and worked out between the lines.

The bullets were pretty thick, and one of my friends, an Italian who had been in on all the parties, was killed near me. The same night Battalion D had four killed and fifteen wounded. The night before, Battalion C lost fifteen. All this was without any real fighting. I hate to think of what is going to happen soon, for we are all going into hard action. A big battle is going to commence soon, and we have already received instructions as to what our position will be in it and what we have got to do. It is no rumor this time. I have

40

seen the troops, artillery, etc., enough to convince me. So in the meantime we are making the best of things and getting the most out of life possible. To-night, we go down to the trenches, I think to stay a couple of days.

I was sorry to hear that some of my letters home had been published, as I do not want any publicity or fame, and do not care to write for the newspapers. This is not a very good letter, but it will have to do for to-day. I will write again soon.

Love,
KIFFIN.

Post Card to the Vicomte du Peloux
May 11, 1915.

DEAR FRIEND:

Am en route to some hospital, having received a nice clean bullet through the thigh day before yesterday.

We made one glorious advance, breaking the German lines, driving them out of the trenches and advancing over open country fighting every step of the way. It lasted for five hours, and by then we had advanced three or four kilometers.

I do not know where I am going, but we are now in Abbeville, so that is on the route to Paris. If we go through there I will try to get off and go to the American Ambulance.

KIFFIN ROCKWELL.

Hôpital Auxiliaire No. 101,
Rennes, I le et Vilain,
May 13, 1915.

DEAR PAUL:

Well, I am lying between two nice, clean sheets now for the first time in nearly nine months, so I guess you know how good it must feel.

We went to the trenches on May 5th to stay forty-eight hours, as the trenches were only a little over one hundred meters apart, and there was nothing to do but stand guard and work building tunnels and *boyaux* toward the German trenches. When our two days were up, instead of being relieved, we were told that there was to be an

41

attack all along that line the coming night at midnight, and that our battalion was to lead our regiment. So all that day, everyone was busy going to the rear for cartridges, food, etc., and also working throwing up an embankment nearly reaching to the barbed wire of the "Boches." This work was very dangerous, as it was done under rifle fire and danger from bombs, but we were protected a little by our own rifle and artillery fire. I spent three hours at it and didn't like it a bit.

We got everything ready, and at eight o'clock settled down to wait for the bombardment which was to precede the attack, but it didn't begin. At ten o'clock, we were told that the attack had been postponed, and that the following morning we would be relieved. So we went out to our temporary trench and spent the night on guard in it. The following morning we were relieved, and marched twelve kilometers to the rear (four of them through trenches).

That night at seven o'clock I lay down thinking I would get a good night's sleep, having had only five or six hours' sleep in the last three days. At one o'clock in the morning, we were awakened and told to make our *sacs* at once. We left in short order, arriving in the second-line trenches at daybreak, where we took our position.

In a few minutes it began to sound as if all hell had broken loose, when our artillery all along the line opened up on the Germans. The d——dest bombardment imaginable was kept up until ten o'clock. Along the whole German line, you could see nothing but smoke and debris. At ten o'clock, I saw the finest sight I have ever seen. It was men from the Premier Étranger crawling out of our trenches, with their bayonets glittering against the sun, and advancing on the Boches. There was not a sign of hesitation. They were falling fast, but as fast as men fell, it seemed as if new men sprang up out of the ground to take their places. One second it looked as if an entire section had fallen by one sweep of a machine-gun. In a few moments, a second line of men crawled out of our trenches; and at seven minutes past ten, our captain called "*En avant,*" and we went dashing down the trenches with the German artillery giving us hell as we went.

Just as we reached the first-line trenches, a shell burst near the captain, and left his face covered with blood. He brushed his hand across it, and I heard him say *"Cochons,"* and that it was nothing. Then he called for everyone out of the trenches.

We scrambled out, and from then on it was nothing but a steady advance under rifle, machine-gun and artillery fire. We certainly had the Boches on the run, but at the same time they were pouring the lead at us. We would dash forward twenty-five or fifty meters, and then when the fire got too hot, would drop to the ground with our *sacs* in front of us, and lie there until we had our breath, and the bullets were not quite so thick. Then we would take our *sacs* in one hand as a kind of shield, and make another dash.

To think of fear or the horror of the thing was impossible. All I could think of was what a wonderful advance it was, and how everyone was going against that stream of lead as if he loved it. I kept that up for five hours. By then we had advanced three or four kilometers, but were badly cut up and also mixed up with men from other regiments, mostly Algerian tirailleurs. Most of our officers had fallen, including the Colonel and three commandants. (I understand that there only remain now four officers out of the whole regiment.) We had taken most of a village and were taking the rest of it. My outfit was a little to the left, and we were being raked by fire from in front and from the end of the village still held by the Germans.

Skipper Pavelka and I were lying alongside the sous-lieutenant when a messenger came and told him that the captain and lieutenant had both fallen, and that he was in command of the company. The fire had been so heavy for the last half hour that we had been advancing one man at a time to the section. The sous-lieutenant gave us the direction to take, and told us to follow him, one at a time. He jumped and dashed forward. I turned to Skipper and told him we might as well get it over with at once, so I started with Skipper behind me.

I go about twenty meters when a bullet catches me in the thigh, through the fleshy part, without touching the bone. I continue for a few steps, and then topple over. Skipper sees me drop, so drops also in order to bandage me up if necessary. But I told him I could do it myself and for him to go ahead. I crawled over to a marmite hole, and into it. There I examined my wound and bandaged it; then turned my attention to a comrade of the 156th Regiment who was lying there. He had been shot through both hips and afterwards a

43

piece of shell had gone through his stomach. I tried to bandage him up, but he was dying and I could not do any good. He wanted water, but I had none and could get none for him. That was the cry going up everywhere, for water. I stayed there until he died.

The line had not advanced any more, and the fire was terrific. While I was lying there, three shells exploded within ten meters of me, each time covering me with dirt. The last one landed within five or six meters of me. I would hear them coming and would say to myself, "Well, it is over," and shut my eyes. Then I would brush the dirt off, and find that I was all right. Finally, I crawled out of the hole, and up to the line where the men were; but they told me to crawl to the rear, saying the Boches might counterattack, and then I would be captured. I knew they were right, so I started snake-fashion for the rear. I made about a kilometer that way to a haystack where there were several other wounded men. It was dark then, so I rested there and put my bandage on again, as it had come off. After a while a Red Cross man came. He told us that there were so many wounded that it would probably be the following day before we could get transported to the rear. So I found a stick and managed to hobble two or three kilometers more to a farm, where there was a large number of wounded.

I slept there that night, and the following morning continued on my way. Finally, by walking some and riding a little on an artillery cart, I got my evacuation card, and at midnight was able to get on a train. It was very crowded, and by the following day my leg was too sore for me to move about much. About midnight we passed through Paris, but no one was allowed to get off. The first stop this side of Paris I was taken off, and I asked to go to Paris. The major said he would send me there, but there was so much confusion that I suppose he got mixed up. Anyway, I was put on a train and instead of going to Paris arrived here last night, and was brought to this hospital this morning.

This is a better hospital than the average, and so I really have no complaint to make. So far, I have been treated royally here. I am in the officers' ward, and have every convenience. I went four days without any attention to my wound (there were so many more badly wounded than I that I did not have the heart to ask for care), and it

44

has festered a little, so they may have to open it up to-night, but it is nothing bad and will soon be all right.

This has been a long letter and I am tired after it. This will do for Monsieur du Peloux also, as it is too much of a task for me to write many long letters. Send me fifty francs, not a *mandat,* but a bill in a registered letter, as it will be more convenient for me. You might also write the *vaguemestre* of my company, telling him that I am wounded and for him-to forward my mail to your address. In that way, I will be more certain of receiving it. When I am well, I will also want you to help me get eight days' *congé* in Paris.

Much love,

KIFFIN.

An afterthought: the Legion has again come into its own. We took the Boche colonel prisoner, this was mentioned in the papers.

To the Vicomte du Peloux

Military Hospital 101,

Rennes,

May 18, 1915.

MY DEAR FRIEND:

I hope you will pardon my not having written you sooner but I knew Paul was telling you I am doing well and I have been a little tired, so have just rested without doing any writing.

I will not write much of the battle as Paul told you what I knew about it and the papers told you more. However, I want to say that I was certainly proud of my regiment that day. When I was in the second regiment I had but little confidence in the men and never wanted to see them called upon to make an attack. When I went into the first regiment I immediately saw that it was composed of different kind of men. They were more serious about the war, and the volunteers were men who engaged out of love and admiration for France, and because they knew they were *right.* They were men who had the courage of their convictions and were willing to die, if necessary, to prove it. So the day we were called upon to attack, every man went into it willingly with the determination to do his best, and humming the Marseillaise. As to the officers—no officers ever led their men better than ours led us. Practically every one of them fell, but they fell at the head of their men, urging them onward.

I don't want you to think that I am cold-blooded, without feeling, but the horror of it all is overshadowed by the feeling of, pride and admiration I have for them all. This life does not hold such great value in my eyes as it does in some people's, and I feel that those men who died that day, died having made a success of their lives in their own little way, doing something for the world, for posterity, and that their characters are their souls which will forever live and be passed down from generation to generation. So, is not that success! And what more can a man ask for his life than success?

As for me—I only have a little old wound through the muscles of the thigh which will probably keep me out of the fight for a couple of months but not pain me much and will allow me to take life easy.

This is a very nice hospital and all are fine to me. There are several nurses who speak English, and they and the English speaking residents of the town come around every day to see me. I am in the office-room and in it also are a sous-lieutenant and a young artilleryman whose father is a colonel in the cavalry. Both speak English. And as I have said, they just all treat me fine. At times it really embarrasses me. Then Paul comes up from twelve until five. I have piles of magazines, books and newspapers to read and all kinds of good things to eat. So you see, I am in a regular paradise here and consider myself exceptionally lucky.

Paul has told me a lot about you and your wife and your kindness to him and seems to be greatly attached to you both. Again, I want to thank you for what you have done for us both. I sincerely hope I may soon have the pleasure of seeing you in Paris.

Sincerely yours,
K. Y. ROCKWELL.

Hospital 101,
Rennes, May 21, 1915.

DEAR MAMMA:

I have wanted to write to you but knew that Paul and the Vicomte du Peloux would write you that I am doing well. My wound

46

is through the muscles of my thigh and doesn't pain me any but will keep me away from the front for at least two months. This is a better hospital than the average and I am treated royally so really rather enjoy it.

Paul is here and comes in every day from twelve to five, and it seems to me that everyone in the city who can speak English has been in to see me, offering to do whatever is possible for me.

They tell me I will be here six or eight weeks and after that I will get at least a week's convalescence in Paris. Then I don't know what I will do. Our depot is in Lyons but there is practically nothing left of my regiment. We did some brilliant work and made a great advance, but naturally suffered terribly in doing so. When I was wounded we had captured all the trenches in front of us, had taken one village, La Targette, and were taking Neuville St. Vaast. Most of my regiment had fallen and I presume that the rest fell during the following days. So when we wounded report for service I suppose we will be put in some other regiment, although I do not know. If they put us into regular French Régiment s I will try to get into one in which the Vicomte du Peloux has officer friends. However, I am hoping that if Italy declares war to-day or to-morrow the war will soon be over. If the U. S. would do right it would end sooner. Germany is sure to lose, but how long the struggle will last is a question.

Paul tells me that when he arrived in Paris he found we were quite well advertised, but not to our advantage, by a number of rather wild letters you had written to everyone you could think of. If you had understood a little more about war and diplomatic affairs, you would have known that the Ambassador could be of absolutely no assistance to us while we were in the army. Then, too, you wrote me a letter of advice as to how I should act if taken a prisoner. I never entertained the idea of being taken a prisoner, but if I had been and had followed your advice, I would have been immediately put up against a tree and shot. Now, we appreciate the fact that your efforts are out of love for us, but there are a lot of things you do not understand in regard to conditions over here and the war, and it is hard for one to give advice about something one does not understand.

It is marvelous to me the way the women of France are doing their share and the courage and fortitude they show.

Much love,

KIFFIN.

To the Vicomte du Peloux

Hospital 101,
Rennes, May 26, 1915.

MY DEAR FRIEND:

I received your letter several days ago and enjoyed and appreciated it. I am taking life exceptionally easy; my wound is progressing well and I suffer very little. Owing to the long time I had gone without attention, they thought at first they would have to cut it open, but it is doing so well they have decided cutting is not necessary.

As I said before, this hospital is much better than the average military hospital. It was a large school for boys before the war. It has a nice garden and on fine days I am carried down to enjoy it. Paul's visits make it a great deal pleasanter for me and I have many other visitors. But I have much time for reading which is mostly English magazines, though I read the French papers every morning. When I get a little more energy I shall devote more time to the French. At present, I am taking my mind off everything as much as possible. Sometimes, I nearly imagine that the whole war has been only a horrible nightmare. But it doesn't take me long to disillusion myself. The hospital has so many pitiful examples of the effects of the war— men crippled and terribly disfigured for life.

I do hope the war will soon be over and that Italy has really come in, which may cause other small nations to join us also. However, I do not want it to end till Germany is completely broken. We have all gone through so much that it would be a shame to have it to do over again in a few years.

There was a Sous-Lieutenant Mallet here who was very kind to me. He has now gone with his mother to Paris. I understand his father is a prominent banker there. Perhaps you know them?

I shouldn't be surprised if Paul returns to Paris soon and I think he'd be more contented there. I think he finds it rather dull in

Rennes.

My kindest regards and love to your wife,

Sincerely yours,

KIFFIN.

Hospital 101,
Rennes, June 8, 1915.

DEAR MAMMA:

Paul went back to Paris Saturday and so I am all alone now. I am still in bed but hope soon to get up. My wound has closed up very nicely but of course the muscles are still rather sore and the side where the bullet came through has to heal over, which will take some time as the hole is rather large.

I received a letter from one of the boys of my squad, telling me what happened after I was wounded. There were six Americans in my squad and eight others of different nationalities. We all fell but the other five Americans and the corporal who was a very good friend of mine. He was a Moor and spoke a little English. The second day of the fighting he took command of the company. Two battalions of about half strength have been formed out of the whole regiment.

We are all watching the U. S. now. If she wants to keep up her name and be respected by other nations, I don't see how she will keep from fighting. If she does declare war it ought to be easy for you to get a good commission for me. If troops were to be sent over here I could stay in France and be quite a lot of assistance when the troops arrive.

I have received but little mail from U. S. since I changed Régiment s. However, the Vicomte du Peloux keeps me posted. Write me in care of him, or of Paul.

Much love,

KIFFIN.

To the Vicomte du Peloux

Hospital 101,
Rennes, June 10, 1915.

MY DEAR FRIEND:

I suppose Paul has told you all the news there is but I will write

49

to let you know I am doing well. I walk a little around the room, not much, however, but I hope soon to be able to go to Paris.

Life is about the same each day with me. I spend the morning reading and in the afternoon I go down into the garden, where I usually have visitors. I try to improve my French a little each day, although I think I make mighty slow progress. I have been a little disappointed in the news lately. I have been hoping and expecting all along that the fighting would end this summer, but I am beginning to fear it will take longer.

I am now watching my own country, but must admit that I have not the great faith in it I probably should have. I was glad to see in the morning's paper that Bryan's resignation has been accepted. I was always an ardent admirer of Bryan until he became Secretary of State. I also thought Mr. Wilson a good man and maybe he still will not disappoint me.

Well, they are waiting to carry me down into the garden. Tell Paul I hope his affairs are progressing nicely.

With best regards to yourself and wife,

Sincerely yours,
KIFFIN.

Hospital 101,
Rennes, June 15, 1915.

DEAR MAMMA:

The Vicomte du Peloux sent me the letter you wrote to me when you first heard I was wounded. I could see by it that you were imagining all kinds of things. In this war, if a rifle bullet doesn't kill one outright he can feel pretty sure of getting well, and in most cases have absolutely no bad effects. When a man gets hit by a rifle bullet he is considered lucky by everyone, himself included. It is only the pieces of shell and the poisonous gases that we are afraid of. The only rest one gets is when he is wounded; so it was really rather welcomed by me, although I am very tired of the hospital now and will be glad to leave it soon.

When you write of the chances of my being killed I can see that you have a great horror of it. But I don't see anything so terrible in death. Of course, anyone with any feeling at all hates to see a loved one or a friend die. I didn't watch a friend of mine continue on after I was wounded because I did not wish to see him if he fell. But if he had fallen I should have felt proud of him because he did his duty and died bravely. So if I should be killed I think you ought to be proud in knowing that your son tried to be a *man* and was not afraid to die, and that he gave his life for a greater cause than most people do—the cause of all humanity. To me that doesn't appear a bad death at all. Otherwise, I may never do anything worthwhile, or any good to anyone after the war, and may live to regret that I wasn't killed in it. So whatever comes I don't want you feeling sorrowful or worrying. And don't be afraid of my taking any foolish chances just to appear brave. I always take every precaution possible and have no desire to be killed by foolishness. Whatever is necessary to be done I try to do conscientiously, but that is all.

Much love for all,

KIFFIN.

Hospital 101,

Rennes (I. et V.),

June 15, 1915.

DEAR PAUL:

There is little to write. I am tired of the hospital and either want to be where I can do as I please or back at the front. It is uncertain when I can get away from this hole. I walk fairly well now and my wound is practically healed, just the muscles a little stiff. There is no reason why I couldn't go to Paris convalescing until all right to go back to the front, except the rules in regard to the wounded. When I leave this hospital, it is necessary for me to go to a convalescence hospital here in town. There it is entirely up to that hospital as to when I leave. They may let me go the first day, or it may be two weeks. They say that that hospital is very poor in food, beds and everything. So as I say, I can't tell when I will get away. They might let me leave here the last of this week, send me to that hospital, where they might let me leave at once. Or I may stay around here a week or two, and afterwards the same length at the other hospital. I don't know whether I will need it or not, but in case of emergency you had better send me some more money in your next letter.

It has been raining the last two days and my rheumatism in my right shoulder has been the worst it ever was, so all in all I haven't been in a very good humor.

The pretty blonde Alsatian comes down to see me every afternoon and I enjoy talking to her very much, as we have become quite friendly, but I declare that the women do not make much impression on me any longer. The Englishman comes often but gets on my nerves.

Haven't received much mail. Had a letter from Weeks and one from Skipper. They say that the Italians in the Legion have all been liberated, that the regiment is very small— only thirty-five in their company, and that they haven't been back in the front-line trenches since the battle. They said that some of the 2ème were up there, but didn't go in the trenches, left for somewhere else.

Hope everything is coming along well with you.

Love,

KIFFIN.

To the Vicomte du Peloux

Hospital 101,

Rennes,

June 19, 1915.

MY DEAR FRIEND:

There is little of interest to write. Your letter of the first of the week is the last mail I have received, so I don't know much of what is going on away from here. I am passing the time about the same as ever; walk very well, though my muscles are still stiff. I had hoped to leave here this week but am told that I will have to stay several days yet before going to the convalescence hospital, where it will depend on the doctor as to how soon I get to Paris. Owing to the uncertainty of the length of time I'll be here you might send me fifty francs. When Paul left I didn't expect to be here long and took but little money from him.

I am about getting resigned to the idea of another winter's campaign and for that reason have decided to accept as long a convalescence as they will give me. I am told here to ask for a month and that I will get it.

I have a notice here from the station to the effect that there are packages there for me weighing thirteen kilos. I suppose they are the packages you sent in May and part of some packages sent from England in March. They have not forwarded my letters to me from the Régiment . I would rather they had sent my letters and have given the packages to my comrades there.

Love to your wife,

Sincerely yours,
KIFFIN ROCKWELL.

Hospital 101,
Rennes, June 20, 1915.

DEAR PAUL:

I have received your letter this morning, for which of course I was glad, as I was wondering why you hadn't written and why I didn't receive any mail at all all week. I don't expect that I can get to Paris before a week at the earliest. I am walking all right now but my muscles are still a little sore. I must have some money, as I don't know what expenses I will have here. What clothes I had on were in very bad condition, and the clothes they give you here are second hand and no good, so I have been having my coat and over-trousers fixed up. The coat was in very bad condition and I gave it in to be washed and mended so that I can wear it.

Two sous-lieut's from *Ban B.* came here wounded yesterday evening. I talked to one of them. He told me that what was left of the regiment (after May 9th) fell this week. He said that he was in B. i. and that when he left the battlefield there were only six left in the company. He said that a lot of things happened that the newspapers haven't told of. He said that we broke a big hole in the German line and that the cavalry came up to carry through the advance, but that fresh infantry did not come up as was intended and for that reason we were unable to go on through and caused the troops there and the cavalry very heavy losses. From his news I can't see how the Americans could escape at least being wounded. You might, when you have the chance, inquire at the American hospital to see if by chance any of them are there, and if so make it a little pleasanter for them. I am writing to-day to Weeks and Pavelka to see if I can get in touch with them.

The last three days have brought a great number of wounded. Yesterday afternoon, one of the wounded had the detonator of a bomb in his pocket which dropped on the floor. One of our fellows in this room stepped on it. It exploded, blowing a hole through his shoe, knocking him over, and a piece entered his leg. Another bit entered the leg of one of the men connected with the hospital, who had never seen the front.

I received part of the stuff Mrs. Coumbe sent us, and a package Madame du Peloux sent me the first of May, yesterday. Nearly everything was spoiled.

I am going out for a walk in the town soon.

Love,
KIFFIN.

Hospital 101,
Rennes, I. et V.,
June 22, 1915.

DEAR PAUL:

I am enclosing you a letter I received this morning from Skipper. I received a card from him also, written before the letter, in which he said that he had been bayoneted, so it was evidently a bayonet that got him as he was fixing to jump on the Boche. It appears that the Regiment was reorganized just before the attack and B. 2 put in with B. 1, the company the sous-lieutenant here is from and of which only six men remained at night time of the 16th.

The Greeks Skipper speaks of were not with us before. I thought they were in the 3eme Régiment de Marche, so perhaps the two regiments were put together just before this last battle. Skipper evidently never received my letter in which I enclosed the "piece of change," so I am sending him five francs to-day to keep him in tobacco until I can send him more, and I want you to do anything you can for him from Paris. Skipper's family didn't amount to anything and he never had any education to speak of, and he has been on his own lookout ever since a child, rambling about the world, but he has the sentiments of a gentleman. He did not have to enlist for France, he could have gotten a boat away from Europe and continued as

54

a sailor. But he is a good lad and brave. He has no way of getting money from home and no friends in France. Now I want you to find someone in Paris who appreciates that a chap like that is fighting for France, and who will take him when he gets his convalescence, so that he can enjoy it before returning to the front. You and I can keep him in spending money, and his wants are simple and few.

As I have already said, the 1er was a good regiment and it makes me sad to hear of so many having fallen. All those he mentions are fine fellows. Nemorin was from India, had studied at Oxford, and was a fine, great-hearted Indian and a good friend of ours. I can always feel proud of having been in the 1er, for they certainly have done their work well.

Write soon.

With love,

KIFFIN.

P. S.   If you can locate Mrs. Weeks you might see if you can find out anything about Kenneth.

Post Card, Postmarked June 24, 1915

Hôpital Convalescence No. 83,

1ère Cie, Rennes, I. et V.

I came to the convalescence hospital to-day. They were going to send me to the depot as I had nothing to show that I could stay in Paris. I put up a holler, so they told me to wire you for a certificate of lodging, signed by the mayor, which I am doing. Send it at once.

KIFFIN.

Post Card, Dated June 27, 1915.

Hôpital Con. 83.

Received the certificate yesterday and passed my last visit. Was given a month's convalescence and am now waiting for them to tell me when to start. I may start tomorrow, or it may be three or four days. Can't tell anything about it. Just have to wait for their convenience to give me my papers.

KIFFIN.

June 27, 1915.

DEAR MAMMA:

Have received two or three letters from you, one from Agnes and one from Irma this week, and enjoyed them all.

I am now in the convalescent hospital here in Rennes and I have been given a month's convalescence in Paris. Am now waiting for my papers before starting.

In regard to what I have done for France—I had rather be fighting for France than doing anything else now. If one is going to fight, I don't see why the *country* should have as great an influence as the *principle*. I am just following out my old theory that we are a part of this whole scheme of affairs and that we can't successfully confine ourselves to one small district. Everyone over here is suffering but the people are growing calmer all the time.

I am in fine health and am looking forward to my stay in Paris.

Much love,

KIFFIN.

Paris, July 8, 1915.

DEAR MAMMA:

I have intended writing every day but am always on the go. I have hardly had a minute to myself since I arrived here. Everyone is lovely to me. I met Paul's fiancée and her mother last week. They are certainly nice people and very influential in France. The Vicomte and Vicomtesse du Peloux are two of the finest people I ever knew and are of the best of the old aristocratic families in France. They seem to think a world of Paul and me, in fact they treat us as if we were their own children. They have lovely apartments and we dine there very often. Last night, they had Prince Colonna to dine with us. He is French and Italian, I think. There is a chance of his cousin being King of Italy sometime. Monday, we are to go out to the American Ambulance with him.

Paris is very sad now and we all wish the war could end, but I have very little hope of that being any time soon because the only peace that would be any good is a peace of complete victory, which will take time, for the Germans are still strong.

I have all this month here but will return to my depot the 1st of

August. You and Agnes must continue to be brave, for every day I am gladder I came over and am fighting for France.

I think Paul will be married before many months, and he has certainly found a fine girl.

Much love,
KIFFIN.

Paris, July 20, 1915.

DEAR MAMMA:

I have been "on the go" too much to write. Paul and I have made many friends over here and have many invitations out. We spend much time with Mrs. Weeks, who is mother of one of my friends in the 1er Régiment, who is missing. Then Pavelka, the American who was with me when I was wounded on May 9th, has been here on a week's convalescence, as he was wounded by a bayonet on June 16th. He has given me full particulars of all that happened between May 9th and June 16th. After May 9th, the Regiment was cited in the order of the army, and then each battalion decorated, and every night long reports read about the bravery of the regiment, etc.

After that, the Regiment was completely re-organized. All the men from the depot were sent up and also a battalion of Greeks. But now after June 16th we get no reports and the nearest I can find out, the regiment doesn't exist any longer as a unit. It appears that I may be sent to the 3rd Reg. de Marche of the 1st Regiment, in Alsace, in a very quiet sector. If I go there I will then have seen all the line in France.

We dine to-morrow night with our friends, the Vicomte and Vicomtesse du Peloux, who take so much interest in us all. They watch for your letters.

Much love,
KIFFIN.

Paris, July 31, 1915.

DEAR MAMMA:

I leave to-night for the depot, after having had a very enjoyable vacation. It was really the first month's vacation I have had, as you know, for five or six years, so I have enjoyed it, especially as

57

everybody has been so nice to me.

I had a long talk with our Ambassador this week. He told me that owing to the letter he received from you he went to the War Department and tried to get Paul and me released. I was awfully sorry to hear that he had done that; but he offered to do anything possible for me. So I asked him to go back to those people and explain things, and tell them I regret that such a request had ever been made. I hope to get a few favors from the War Department now, so I want to fix things with them.

Paul is well and expects Mademoiselle Jeanne here in a few days. The Vicomte left to-day for the country. I have spent much of my time here with Mrs. Weeks whose son was with me north of Arras, and who has been missing since June 16th. She is very brave and we all hope Kenneth is a prisoner. He was a nice fellow, only twenty-five years old, and had written six or seven books that had been published.

Mrs. Weeks told me she was going to write to you.   I do not know what my address will be, so write me care of Paul.

Much love,

KIFFIN.

1er Régiment Étranger,

2ème Rég't de Marche,

5ème Cie.,

Dépôt de Lyon,

Sunday, Aug. 1, 1915.

DEAR PAUL:

Well, I arrived here all o. k. this morning and spent the morning getting settled. Conditions don't look very good. The place is filthy dirty and they say rotten food, but tomorrow morning I am going to the doctor and ask for electric treatment. I understand that if I get that I will be exempt from all service and allowed to go out from one until nine. I will try to keep that up until I find out just what is coming of the different propositions and then if they can't come through I will leave for the front.

I only found one man here that I know. He was in my squad and shot through the shoulder. Every time I inquire after anyone they say "dead," except Kenneth Weeks and the other boys. No one seems to know. But I was told that we lost ground on June 16th, and that the Colonel's orderly was taken prisoner after being wounded in the leg. He lost his leg and has already been sent back (from Germany) and I hope to get his address to-morrow, and maybe he can give me some information.

Thierry-Delanoe left for Paris two days ago. Grumet is in the country for a week or so, so I am all alone. It is true that all the Legion is all together, and we even have men here from the Dardanelles. My corporal was wounded there. I expect I will see Trinkard to-morrow. As I have no one to write French for me, will send you the name of the Commandant here: Lt.-Colonel Metz, Commandant du Dépôt, 1ᵉʳ Régt. Étranger, Lyon. You can either send his name to Monsieur Leygues, or write a letter in French for me to send to him.

Well, this is about all to write. Keep up good spirits and give our friends my regards.

Much love,
KIFFIN.

To Mrs. Alice Weeks.
Lyon, Sunday, Aug. 1, 1915.

MY DEAR GOOD, SWEET SECOND MOTHER:

I read your letter last night on the train and it did make me feel much better and happier. But I spent, I think, the saddest night in my life. I was not sad because I was going back to the war, but it was from thinking of the ones who stay behind. I was in a second-class coach and very comfortable but I could not sleep. I just thought and thought all night long and could not keep the tears out of my eyes. I want to live now more than I ever did in my life, but not from the selfish standpoint. This war has taught me many things, and now I want to live to do whatever good is possible. But if I am killed at any time during the war I will not be afraid to die, and you may know that I will die like a man should, feeling that it is the greatest death that a man can die. I will always take the greatest care of myself and not do foolish things, but will always try to do my duty to the utmost for what we are fighting for.

Paul feels it very much that he can't go back to the front but he is really not strong enough and couldn't possibly do it. So I wish you'd rather look after him and keep his spirits up as much as possible; and whatever comes, don't let him come back.

I arrived at the Caserne about eight o'clock this morning and spent an hour or more getting settled. Things do look very bad and I wouldn't want to stay here very long. But to-morrow I am going to report to the Doctor and ask for electric massage for my thigh because it really needs it. I think by that I can have things my own way and go out from one till nine P.M. and also not do any work. If I can do that, it will not be so bad, and I will soon be changed, or returned to the front.

I saw only one man that I knew but I was so glad to see him that I took him out to lunch with me. I don't think much of him but the poor fellow has no money and hasn't had any convalescence, so it was a chance to make him a little happier.

I have heard that our Regiment lost a number of prisoners June 16th and one man—orderly to the Colonel—was taken prisoner and lost his leg and has already been returned to France. I hope to get his address to-morrow and maybe he can give me some information about Kenneth. They say that most of the men taken prisoner were wounded, but we will hope for the best.

After lunch, I went to the hospital to look up a friend, but he left two days ago for Paris. Then I went to the home of a boy who was in the hospital at Rennes with me. He left this morning for the country to stay a week or two. So I am all alone, sitting in a café writing to you, and I shall write other letters.

It is true that the two regiments are put together now.

Well, keep cheerful and in good hopes, and I will also.

With much love,

KIFFIN.

1er Rég. Étranger,
2ème Rég. de Marche.
5ème C[ie.],
Dépôt de Lyon.

LETTERS FROM THE FOREIGN LEGION

1er Étranger,
5ème Cie.,
Lyon, Friday,
Aug. 6, 1915.

DEAR PAUL:

There is no news to write, as I have done absolutely nothing since being here. Just go to the assembly and for a walk each day, escorted by the sergeant. There is nothing to do in the town also. I get out from five until nine, and try to take up as much of that time as is possible eating dinner. I am thoroughly demoralized, as far as this outfit goes. Every single nationality that is engaged in this war is being released; except the ones who might be Germans, Austrians or Turks: they are being sent to Africa. The ones that will be left will be a rotten bunch. If by any chance I am not transferred to the aviation, they ought at least to put me in a French regiment.

Sunday, a detachment leaves for La Valbonne. I think I will go with it. That is only thirty kilometers from here and I think will be better. I will have to drill there, but if I stay here, my eight days repose I was given will be up, and I will have to work all the time.

Trinkard is here, but is in another company, in another building. I see him once in a while in the evening. He said that Hubmajer, the big Serbian, passed through here on his way to Serbia. By the way, I was looking over the list of punishments here and found Carl Jean Drossner down for two years hard labor for desertion.

Well, give everyone my regards.

Love,
KIFFIN.

1er Étranger,
1ère Cie.,
La Valbonne,
Sunday (Aug. 8, 1915).

DEAR PAUL:

Just a line to let you know that I came here this morning with the detachment that left Lyon. I found Pavelka all right, and Trinkard came with me; then there is also another American here. I don't think it is so bad here. It is a little like Camp Mailly, only I think better.

There are plenty of cafes in the small town here, and a canteen in the camp. The room that I am in is very clean and I have a sleeping bag, clean blanket and all, and am feeling better all around except I am still hoping the transfer will come through this week.

Am now in a cafe having a drink with the boys.

Much love,
KIFFIN.

To the Vicomte and Vicomtesse du Peloux
1er Rég't Étranger,
1ère Cie.,
La Valbonne,
Aug. 10, 1915.

MY DEAR FRIENDS:

I will address my letters to you both. I should have written earlier but have not been doing anything since coming back, and also haven't really known what address to give. All last week was spent in Lyon, didn't do any exercises or work while there, just stayed around the caserne which was formerly a school. It was very dirty there and everything was so as to get a person rather demoralized. So Sunday, when a detachment came here, I came also. This is only thirty kilometers from Lyon. It is a regular military camp right out in the country. The sleeping quarters are good and there is plenty of fresh air, trees and grass. So I like it here. To-morrow, I will have to start in on the exercises. All of the Legion in France is now in one regiment, and a couple of men who were with me in the 2eme Regiment are here now, and Pavelka is here. They are sending all the men who may be Germans, Austrians or Turks to Africa and are liberating all the Russians, Italians, Belgians, English, etc. —who can go to their own country or into a French regiment. The Greeks are all being sent to the Dardanelles. So what will be left of the Legion here will as a whole be a rather poor lot, because most of the men who stay will be men who can't possibly go elsewhere. I haven't heard anything encouraging about getting something better, but am still hoping.

I can't tell how long I will be here before going to the front, but know that it will be some time.

I hope you are both enjoying the country.

Sincerely yours,

KIFFIN.

To Mrs. Alice Weeks

La Valbonne,

Thursday (Aug. 12, 1915).

MY DEAR SECOND MOTHER:

Just a note to let you know how happy I am.

I have really not done anything since I have come here and this is not a bad place but it is "in the air" for everyone to be demoralized—officers and men. Yesterday afternoon, I was to the point of not caring about anything or what happened, when Pavelka came over to where I was. He had just been called up about the aviation. In a few minutes they were around looking for me. I went to the bureau and found that an order had come in to transfer the two Legionnaires, Pavelka and Rockwell, to the aviation corps. We were so happy that last night we got several of the boys together and had a regular celebration. This morning, Pavelka and I were busy signing papers at the bureau and passing the medical visit to see if we were all right. Now we are just waiting for the order to move.

You can't imagine how I thank you for all you have done, for I certainly wanted to get out of this place. Yet I don't want you to think I am selfish and only thinking of myself. I have been thinking of you and of Kenneth all the time, and only wish there were something I could do for you. One never receives all one's mail in this regiment and my mail has not come from Lyon. So I don't know whether or not you have received the letter I wrote you, enclosing the address of the corporal who had been a prisoner. In your next letter let me know, and if you have seen him, did he have any news?

Pavelka received your groceries and we enjoyed them very much. As soon as I move I will send you my new address. Don't write here as there is small chance the letter would be forwarded. I hope we will be sent where you can come to see us.

With much love,

KIFFIN.

63

1ᵉʳ Étranger,
(La Valbonne),
Sunday, Aug. 15, 1915.

DEAR PAUL:

I haven't heard from you this week, but Mrs. Weeks wrote me that Jeanne had arrived, so suppose you have been busy. If you have written suppose the letter has been lost like most of my mail. I don't seem to have any luck in receiving my mail since being here. However, I am hoping to leave soon, as Wednesday, the Regiment received a notice from the War Dept. regarding transferring Pavelka and me to the aviation. But they haven't seemed to have sense enough to know what to do and it took them until to-day to get my papers fixed up. I suppose everything is fixed now and hope that in a day or two I will be removed, although can't tell.

There is really not much hard work to do here, and plenty of cafes right in the camp, but it seems to be in the air for everyone to be completely demoralized and it is nothing but grumbling and yelling from morning to night. Prison sentences are handed out freely on the slightest pretext.

As I say, my mail hasn't been arriving at all. I wrote Pechkoff about trying to locate his things. Ask him if he received the letter. I also wrote to Mile, du B.—but didn't know whether I had the address right or not. I am not going to write anyone else until I know just where I am going to be.

Hope everything is going well. Mrs. Weeks said she hoped you were going to take a room at her new apartment. I think that a good idea, as you would be more contented.

Give everyone my regards.

With much love,
KIFFIN.

1ᵉʳ Étranger,
4ᵉᵐᵉ Cⁱᵉ,
La Valbonne,
Thursday (Aug. 26, 1915).

DEAR PAUL:

Just got in this morning from twenty-four hours of trench life.

Yesterday morning, they took the company out at daybreak. It was awfully hot and the company worked all day long digging trenches. Trinkard, another fellow and I volunteered to be the cooks and we had it pretty easy on the rear until eleven o'clock last night when they came and got us and made us go up with the company and work the rest of the night. For the company it was twenty-four hours of steady work with three hours rest in the middle of the day and one hour at midnight, and then the regular hourly ten-minute repose. All to teach them how to make trenches and how to live in them, most of us knew more about it through experience than the officers did. This afternoon we go out for bayonet exercise and grenade throwing.

This morning I received your two letters and one from Mrs. Weeks, written Monday. I doubt if you will be able to do much. What I would like to see is the Legion broken up, as it is a shame and a disgrace to the country the way conditions are now. It has never been any good in this war, except the ones who were killed or wounded on May 8th and June 16th. As far as I can find out, it didn't cover itself with glory the i6th, for what I hear is that Bon B., which went out on the lead, was the only Bon that marched well, and I don't think any of it came back.

I will tell you a few incidents that happened recently:

Two days ago the Commandant passed a review of the men proposed for the *reforme*. Nearly all of them had been wounded, the only one not was Krogh, who is proposed owing to heart trouble. All of the men had been in the trenches all winter. Because these men were going to get out of it through the doctors, the Commandant was sore as hell. He lined them up, some of them could hardly walk, and cursed them out. He told them they were not worth a——— that they disgraced the Legion, and that they only came here for *la gamelle*. Now, we have heard that from sergeants and such all the time. But for a Commandant to tell men who have ruined themselves for life out of a love for France and the principles she is fighting for, I think it is going a little too far.

The same day, August 25th, Sergeant Bergeron, 2eme Cie., went up to a Greek volunteer who could not speak French, and began to curse him about something or other. The Greek could not answer him but just stood at attention. The sergeant kept on talking, and

65

finally hit the Greek twice in the face, knocking him down. The Greek got an interpreter and went to the bureau to *réclame,* but they only laughed at him.

My corporal is a Greek about twenty-one years old. He served through the Balkan wars, coming out a sergeant. He was wounded twice in them, once a revolver bullet, the other time a bayonet. He enlisted here at the outbreak of the war, was a *2ème classe* May 9th, when he was in the first line of men out of the trenches. He was the only man in his squad that didn't fall May 9th, and was named Corporal a few days afterwards. On June 16th, he was wounded, but left the hospital as soon as possible, came here and asked to return at once to the front. They said he was not well enough, and kept him there. He sleeps next to me. Three nights ago he didn't sleep a wink, owing to toothache. The following morning he reported sick. The doctor gave him *consultation motivée,* but didn't exempt him from exercise. To report sick he had to miss the morning exercise. They have a rule now that if you report sick and are not given *exempt service* you go to prison for eight days. This morning they read out eight days prison for the corporal. He took it badly, telling me that he had never before in his military career served a half-hour's prison sentence. He came back here, and I held his coat, while he cut his stripes off. On his way to the prison he carried the stripes and threw them on the floor at the bureau, and told them he wouldn't have them.

Now here is what happens in case you are *exempt service:* The other day, Trinkard sprained his thumb at exercise. He went to the Dr. and the Dr. gave him *exempt service.* He was immediately carried to a room, where all the men *exempt service* are gathered. There they are kept all day until time to turn in at night, with a guard over them. They are not allowed to leave the room and have to listen to Theory all day.

Now, since I have been here, there has been no one that has said a word out of the way to me. Yet I see these things every day and never know when my turn will come. And it is such a disgrace to France for such things to happen that I wish something could be done to stop it. My idea is that the Legion should be broken up, and any man France is unwilling to accept in a regular corps be given his freedom. I can't help but believe that if enough of these facts get to the War Department that this will happen.

Well, none of my letters nowadays are anything but complaints, and you know the kind of spirit I was in when I came back.

I am glad that you are with Mrs. Weeks and that you like it; it is much better than living in an hotel.

Regards to our friends.

Much love,
KIFFIN.

To the Vicomte and Vicomtesse du Peloux
La Valbonne, Aug. 29, 1915.

MY DEAR FRIENDS:

Well, I am still in Valbonne doing the same thing each day—drilling—which grows monotonous. I suppose Paul has told you that I came very close to being transferred to the aviation corps. The order came for the transfer but they didn't like to let men out of the Legion, so they kept delaying until they fixed it so I can't go unless a second order comes.

I am now planning to try to go to the Dardanelles with the next detachment. I think the Legion there is pretty good as I have heard fine reports of their actions. Then it would be an interesting trip as I would go from here to Algeria and stay a week in Sidi Bel-Abbès before going to the Dardanelles. It has been very hot here and I never have ambition enough to go out of the camp except on Sundays. There are several cafes in the camp where we can get food and drink. I go there twice a day for an hour or so and sleep the rest of the time that I am not out to exercise. I forgot to write you that when I arrived in Lyon I found that your friend had left the hospital. I know nothing of news.

Sincerely yours,
KIFFIN.

WAR LETTERS OF KIFFIN YATES ROCKWELL

1er Étranger, 4ème Cie.,

La Valbonne,

Sept. 1, 1915.

DEAR PAUL:

Just came in this morning from another twenty-four hours of work and no sleep in the trenches. That is a better idea than the kind of drilling we had last fall, but I get tired of it, after having had the seven months of the real thing.

I suppose Mrs. Weeks has told you of the good news Pavelka got, of Kelly having written his father about being a prisoner. I think that it is pretty sure that Kenneth and Smith are prisoners also. It would be more trouble to get a letter to France from Germany than to the U. S., and then Kenneth may still be in Belgium, where they are not allowed to write. I can't understand why "Red" Scanlon didn't write me or Mrs. Weeks one, as he had both of our addresses. But then he is a slow thinker anyway. Pavelka has written to him and maybe he will send some news in a few days. Then I wrote Mr. Kelly as soon as I got to Lyon and ought to be getting an answer soon. The letter will come to Paris, and if you receive it you open it before forwarding it on to me.

There is not much doing here. I will leave sometime between now and the 15th for the front, not later than the 15th, if I am not transferred before then. I can't tell anything about what they are going to do, so don't know whether it will be for the Dardanelles or this front. If I go to the Dardanelles will go to Algeria first and spend one week at Sidi Bel-Abbès before going on. I suppose I have enough money to last me the rest of the time here but you had better send me about 250 francs for emergencies, because if I were to leave for the Dardanelles, the Lord knows when I would get any more mail. I received Uncle Jake's letter last week. He said that we could draw on his bank for whatever we needed and that he had arranged with mamma to take care of our account.

Have written two letters to the Vicomte du Peloux but received no answer. Did you get my letter last week? I put up such a howl that was afraid they might open it and not send it. I have reached my old point of indifference now, and it doesn't make much difference to me where I go or what I do. I will get along all right wherever they put me.

I expect a day's *permission* in Lyon some time this week. It will be a relief from this place. My regards to all.

Much love,

KIFFIN.

In the same envelope was enclosed the following:
Aviation Militaire,
Division M. Farman,
Avord (Cher).

DEAR PAUL:

Well, at last I am all right. Saturday morning I was just going on guard when the Adjutant came and told me that a telegram had come and that I was to leave in one hour. I went to Lyon and there got my papers and finished up with the Legion. I was to have left Saturday night, at eight-fifteen, but I was feeling so good that I decided to celebrate, which I did. I left Lyon at five o'clock yesterday morning. Had to change trains four times and arrived at the station here at nine last night.

This is a big camp and is about two kilometers from the station. There were two small hotels there and I tried to get a room for the night, but they were full. So I came out to the camp and spent the night at the *Poste de Police.* Then reported to the bureau this morning. Everything was fine. The Captain shook hands with me and was exceptionally pleasant. He asked me what machine I would like to fly. I didn't know much difference, but he told me that the Maurice Farman was one of the best and easy to learn. So I said all right. I have been getting located this morning and begin work this afternoon, when the Chief Pilot will take me up for a look around.

I suppose you have written me at La Valbonne, and I am writing to-day for my mail. I will probably want you to send me some clothes soon, but don't know what I can get here so will wait.

This is such a relief to be out of the Legion that I can hardly believe it. I think that if I had had to stay at La Valbonne for a month or so longer I would have gone completely "nutty."

Well, I am going out to eat now.

Much love,

KIFFIN.

CHAPTER III

Letters from the Aviation

Élève Pilote Aviation Militaire,
Avord (Cher),
Sept. 8, 1915.

DEAR MAMMA:

Have been very busy lately and now have time for only a note.

I have at last gotten what I have been trying to get these past two months. I am transferred to the aviation as a student-pilot. That is a jump from the lowest branch of the military service to the highest. It is the most interesting thing I have ever done, and is the life of a gentleman, and I am surrounded by gentlemen.

I have been here only this week but I fly each morning and afternoon with an instructor sitting behind me, directing my movements. It is very easy to fly but I must get the habit of the movements, and understand the air currents.

I am perfectly satisfied here and everyone treats me royally.

Love to Agnes and all friends.

Much love,
KIFFIN.

LETTERS FROM THE AVIATION

To the Vicomte and Vicomtesse du Peloux

Aviation Militaire,
Avord, Sept. 8, 1915.

DEAR FRIENDS:

Just a note to let you know that I have at last got what I have been wanting. I am perfectly contented now. Arrived here Monday morning and everyone has been lovely to me. They have immediately started to teach me to fly. I was up for two trips Monday. My instructor is a very nice man and a friend of Casey, one of the Americans of the 2ᵉᵐᵉ Étranger. We go up each morning and afternoon. I sit in front and run the machine while he directs my movements from the rear. It is very easy and most interesting. There are four of us on the same machine, one lieutenant and one sous-lieutenant, one corporal and myself. All of us were north of Arras, May 9ᵗʰ. Am very busy now getting settled and acquainted.

Sincerely,
KIFFIN.

Élève-Pilote, École M. F.,
Camp d'Avord (Cher),
Friday, Sept. 10, 1915.

DEAR PAUL:

Well, I am getting along fine. It is very easy and I take to it just like a duck to water. My instructor is a marvel and an exceedingly nice fellow; he is a friend of Casey's and takes special pains with me. I think he will turn me loose this afternoon and let me fly alone. I am now on a 1913 model Maurice Farman, after I am turned loose will stay on it for four or five days practice and then change to the 1914 model. Will stay on it two or three weeks and then hope to pass my *brevet militaire,* which will entitle me to go to the front. However, afterwards, I think I will ask to change to a Caudron, the same machine that Thaw flies. That would keep me here two or three weeks longer and give me more practice. Then, after leaving here I will have to go to the camp at Paris where we saw Bill (Thaw) and Hall. Will stay there three weeks before going to the front. I can get permission at any time to go to Paris but don't think I will, at least not before I pass my *brevet militaire.*

Most of the *elèves* are lieutenants and sous-lieutenants. There is nothing *militaire* about the life and all the aviators are treated the same. The only difference is the officers wear stripes on their uniforms and are paid more. We all go out on the field at four-forty in the morning and assist in moving the machines out of the hangars. Then we see that the motors, etc., are in good condition. Then we go out on the field and take turns flying with the instructors. At seven o'clock we come in for a little breakfast. At eight, we have a lecture on flying, then go out and put the machines back in the hangars. We are free until nine-thirty. At eleven, we have *dejeuner*. Then we usually sleep until three-thirty, when we go back on the field. We are out there then until after dark. Don't have dinner until eight or after. That is the day's routine. They are all a quiet bunch, little foolishness going on, and all intent on learning to fly as quickly as possible.

I am sending notes and cards now to all our friends. Expect to go to Bourges next week and buy a uniform, cap, large suit-case, gloves and other things of the kind. You might go to the bank and draw some money and send me.

Much love,
KIFFIN.

Élève Pilote, École M. F.,
Camp d'Avord (Cher),
Wednesday, Sept. 15, 1915.

DEAR PAUL:

Was glad to get your letter and the money this evening. To-morrow morning I am going to ask to go to Bourges in the middle of the day and will see what kind of a uniform I can get there. In regard to the clothes you mentioned, send them all, and send me two shirts, also the *passe-montagne* and the scarf, because one of the first things I will do toward gaining my *brevet* will be to mount 2,000 meters in the air and stay there for an hour, and it is cold up there. I wear a *passe-montagne* now when I fly but it isn't much good, and I was going to buy one to-morrow but will not now. Send all the things right away, for I have practically nothing at present.

I am getting along well, although yesterday and to-day have

been bad and we have done nothing each afternoon. I go up now all alone and to-morrow will go on a new machine and begin to go a little higher in the air than I have so far.

In regard to photographs, there is no place here to have them taken. I have had my uniform changed three times since leaving Paris, but still retain the kepi as a souvenir.

What did you write Mamma about her coming over here?

I haven't heard from Mrs. Weeks for a long time. Hope she is all right. Have you heard any more news from any of the boys? And did you get any more news of Scanlan and whether or not he is still in the hospital at Orleans?

Much love,

KIFFIN.

Élève-Pilote, École M. F.,
Camp d'Avord (Cher),
Sunday, Sept. 19, 1915.

DEAR PAUL:

Well, I have finished with the 1913 model Farman and to-morrow I go on the 1914 model and with no bad luck will try to pass my *brevet militaire* during the next two weeks. If I succeed in doing that I will then go to Paris on six days' permission, as that is given to all the men when they finish.

I have been to Bourges twice this week getting things. I couldn't find a ready-made uniform to suit me, so am having one made. It is black, with the broad red artillery stripes on the trousers and I think will look very nice. The kepi is black with red stripes, and then there is a police-bonnet, black with a red stripe. It will all be ready for me Wednesday, and I will go for it then or Thursday, as I want to have it to wear when I start on my different trips for passing my *brevet.* One of the trips is to go to Chartres, 150 kilometers from here, and go in a straight line as the crow flies.

At present I am only a *2ème classe soldat* and *elève-pilote;* as soon as I pass my *brevet militaire* I shall be named corporal as that goes with the *brevet.* After I pass my *brevet* I will change to another machine, probably the Caudron. If so, I will only be here two or three weeks on it before being ready to go to the front. There is a chance of my being named sergeant here in the rear, as I stand in very strong with the officers. If not, you are always named sergeant during the first month at the front. Of course, I hope that I will be able to gain my stripes as a sous-lt, in a little while.

When I came back here I had absolutely nothing; even my toothbrush, poste and comb were stolen from me at La Valbonne, and my dirty clothes were in the wash. I have bought such things as can be found, but am anxiously waiting for the package I asked you to send me. As far as luxuries go, I am able to buy good cigarettes, and wine with my meals, and sometimes eat out at a cafe where good meals are served. But I am not living a riotous life here; I stick close to the camp all the time, and am trying to pass my *brevet* as soon as possible, as I expect to reap the good times after once being at the front.

Answer this immediately. I want to go to Bourges not later than Thursday and get everything I need, as that will probably be the last day that I shall have the time.

Much love,

KIFFIN.

To the Vicomte and Vicomtesse du Peloux
Military Aviation,
Camp d'Avord,
Sept. 19, 1915.

MY DEAR FRIENDS:

Everything is going well with me but I don't feel like writing much these days. I guess I am too busy thinking about all the new things I am learning.

I have been flying all alone this week on the 1913 model Maurice Farman, but to-morrow morning I go on the 1914 model. I will spend only a few days on it in order to get used to it and then will start on the different flights that are necessary for me to pass my *brevet militaire*. They consist of the following:

Stay for one hour or longer two thousand or more meters in the air; make a trip in the form of a triangle to two different towns about sixty or seventy-five kilometers from here; volplane to the ground from a height of 500 meters; and the last is to fly to Chartres in a straight line, over 150 kilometers. I hope with good luck to pass all those tests within the next two weeks.

I seldom go outside the camp, although I went to Bourges twice this week in the middle of the day. I was over there seeing about getting some clothes, as I have more demand for them in the Aviation than I did in the Legion.

I have found some very congenial people here but, so far, have not tried to make any intimate friends. There is here a very nice young boy, only nineteen years old, who is very bright and knows much about aviation. He has just passed his *brevet militaire* at the end of twenty-one days, which is the record. A sous-lieutenant and I fly the same machine but I don't like it much. Sometimes when there is work to be done he is a little inclined to shirk his share of it, and he thinks he knows a great deal more than he really does. But then he isn't a bad fellow.

I hope to be in Paris on permission in a few weeks and will see you then.

My best wishes to you both.

Sincerely yours,

KIFFIN.

To Mrs. Alice Weeks

Wednesday, Sept. 22, 1915.

MY DEAR AUNT ALICE:

I was glad to receive your two letters this week and enjoyed them, also the clippings you sent. I think the clipping about Bryan and the desk was especially good.

You asked me if I was glad that I came into the Aviation. Of course I am glad, but I will be still gladder when I finish here and go to the front as an aviator. I worry more or less here and am not satisfied with everything. We have not got enough machines and there is not enough attention paid to the machines. We have had a great number of machines broken lately and, at present, everything is tied up waiting for them to be put in condition. Yesterday, there were altogether nine machines smashed. I was unlucky enough to be one of the nine. Monday morning I went on the double command 1914 model and made three short tours lasting in all fifteen minutes.

My instructor told me I was very good and there was no need of my continuing under the double command. I was well pleased as I had expected to spend two days under it, as that is the average. I immediately began to count on making my one hour at two thousand meters to-day and finishing my *brevet* by next Monday or Tuesday. Instead, I went in and asked for a machine, but was informed that there were so many broken I would have to wait for one to be repaired. I did nothing Monday afternoon or yesterday until 4:30. The mechanics had been working all day on a machine whose wheels were not good and whose motor did not work well. I was anxious to get started so they told me I could take it out and try it if I wished, but to be careful. I barely got started on the ground when it began to turn with me. I tried to straighten it but could not and saw that it was going to break if I didn't do something, so I tried to get off the ground. The motor, was not working strong enough, so it only made matters worse and threw it completely around, breaking it up pretty badly. It made me awfully mad. Although it was not my fault it does not help my record any and also delays me for several days, as I must now wait for another machine. But it will all come out eventually. I am all right when up in the air, but as our machines are old and not very good, they are hard to manage on the ground.

Much love,

KIFFIN.

École M. F.
Camp d'Avord (Cher),
Monday (Sept. 27, 1915).

DEAR PAUL:

The last week has been practically a week lost for me. We have had bad luck and bad weather. The last flying we have had at all was Friday morning and it was an unlucky morning, as we had three men killed and one badly injured. Two of the deaths were very horrible. It was one of the instructors on a Morane aëroplane and a mechanic. They started out to the end of the field to an accident. On the way a puff of wind caught the aëroplane and almost upset it, then something went wrong and it shot straight up in the air, then fell. The instructor and the mechanic were imprisoned in the wreckage and there was an explosion and the whole mass went up in flames, and they were burned alive with all the men watching but unable to do a thing. In all, last week was very bad, and even if the weather had been good the last two or three days, it wouldn't have made any difference, as I have no machine. I hope to-morrow to have one, but there will probably be five or six of us on it, as there are twelve of us ready to begin our *épreuve* for *brevet,* and all are waiting for *appareils.* I went to Bourges and got my clothes, and feel much better now; also received the package of clothes, which came at an opportune time, as I was in need.

An American named Chapman, from the 3eme de Marche, arrived here this morning and seems to be a very fine fellow indeed. I suppose Skipper and the other boys are fighting, as they had written that they expected to attack.

Much love,

KIFFIN.

Victor Chapman wrote his father, under date of Sept. 27, 1915:

". . . I find a compatriot I am proud to own here. A tall lanky Kentuckian, called Rockwell. He got his transfer about a month ago from the Legion. He was wounded on the 9th of May, like Kisling. In fact, one half of the *2eme* de Marche, 2,300, were wounded that day, not counting the killed and missing. He gives much the best account I have heard. Having charged with the 3rd Battalion and being wounded in the leg on the last *bouck,* he crawled back across the entire field in the afternoon. At this moment I have mixed feelings of pride, envy and sorrow, for he has just received a postal from a friend who has returned to the Regiment. They were given a banner, and three days ago they were up where the big advance took place. On account of their reputation and the general understanding that they were reserved for attack, the Regiment must have been in the very thick of it, and has enormous losses. Even Rockwell is chafing because he changed too soon.

"There is nothing like it, you float across the field, you drop, you rise again. The sack, the 325 extra rounds, the gun, have no weight. And a ball in the head and it is all over—no pain."

To the Vicomte and, Vicomtesse du Peloux

Aviation Militaire, Avord,

Oct. 7, 1915.

MY DEAR FRIENDS:

Last week and this week I have had little to do, as we have had bad weather most of the time. It is now real cold and there has been a heavy mist all morning which has prevented flying. The few times that the weather has permitted flying I have been able to do but little, owing to most of our machines being broken or the motors not working well. Yesterday was fine for flying and I was out on the field at day-break with everything ready to start right in, but the motor would not work. The mechanics worked over it for two hours and got it so we thought it would work all right. I got in, but when I got four hundred meters in the air my motor began to do all kinds of stunts, making a terrible noise, and finally stopped. Luckily I was where I could make a good descent, but I was not at all pleased. They decided that the motor was just tired out from age and usage, so I didn't fly any more for the day and still haven't an *appareil.*

Everybody is fine here but they are really not serious enough and the *appareils* are nearly all old and unsafe. Everyone has been trying to go too fast and do things before having enough training. As a result, we have had a great number of regrettable accidents. Yesterday afternoon, one of the best acquaintances I had here was killed. He was from Paris, spoke good English and was the first man I knew here, and was always very kind and nice to me. We learned on the same machine and he was turned loose on the 1914 model about an hour before I was. He started then on a good *appareil* and flew every time the weather permitted, whereas I have not been able to do so. Yesterday afternoon, he started here from Chartres and almost twenty kilometers from there his body and his machine were found in a mass of wreck. It was undoubtedly the fault of the *appareil* but nevertheless everyone admits that he had not had enough experience flying around the camp before starting out. Yet he was only trying to do what I and the others have been trying to do—that is, finish as soon as possible. Now I think I will go a little slower, as that is the fifth death recently.

At the front one thinks little of a death because there is always more or less glory in it, and we feel that it is necessary there. Here, there is no glory in it, and it seems so unnecessary.

I am afraid that the Legion is "done for," as I got a card from Pavelka, written the 23rd, saying they were to attack in a day or so; and also that the Regiment was in Champagne right where the hottest fighting has been. It has evidently been a glorious advance but I know what those things mean and I feel rather sorry that they tried it unless they continue to advance; and the last two days' reports appear as if they have stopped, like we did.

It is awfully long and hard and there is a lot of time now when I feel completely tired out with it all, but still I am willing to stick it out to the finish.

There is another American here with me now, a very nice fellow who was in the 3eme de Marche of the 1er Étranger.

Will close now. With kindest regards to both.

Sincerely yours,

KIFFIN.

Élève Pilote,
École M. F.,
Camp d'Avord (Cher),
Tuesday, Oct. 5, 1915.

DEAR PAUL:

I was glad to get your letter Sunday and to-day. I knew that the Legion was in the action in Champagne and had expected that it had been badly cut up but had received no word from the boys. I had given them your address as my permanent one, and suppose that the ones who are left will write to one of us there. I am afraid that it has gone badly with Skipper, for otherwise I think he would have written by now.

Thorin is a fine boy. He is a little rough, as he has done nothing but knock around over the world, but he has a good heart and one could not find a better comrade in a fight. He was shot through both legs, jaws and his hand cut open while fighting in Mexico. I found him with Skipper at La Valbonne, anxious to get to the front. I liked him, and when he left for the front gave him a little money. As soon as he writes, send him some money, and also send me his letter so I can write him.

I am doing little or nothing here now. We have first one thing and then another to keep us from flying, mainly bad weather and broken *appareils*. To show you how bad the latter is, there were forty-four good *appareils* in the M. Farman school not long ago, whereas now there are only sixteen. There have been two more fellows killed since I last wrote. One of them was a Jew but a nice fellow. He had been on the same *appareils* that I was on. I was going to do my hour at 2,000 meters Sunday afternoon, but there had been two of us on the same *appareil* and the other fellow broke it when we had only one more flight each to make, before going to the 2,000. So now I am waiting and when I do fly again I will have to go up a few times to get back the practice.

You had better send me some more money. I don't like to keep asking for money, but have to spend more or less here, especially when I am not doing anything, otherwise the life would get too much on my nerves. Then it is always best to have a good sum on you, as sometimes the men flying away from the camp have accidents and stay at some town as long as a week, all the time waiting for repairs, and then you live at an hotel, paying all your own expenses. In regard to magazines, I have been thinking of asking you to send me some, but have always expected to be able to finish most any time and then go to Paris. It is possible for me to finish now this week if everything were exceptionally lucky for me, but I may be kept here two or three weeks longer; can't tell.

According to Mr. Kelly's letter, it is not sure that Russell Kelly is a prisoner, as he has heard nothing since the 16th June.

Chapman got a card from one of his friends of the 3eme de Marche that he was wounded, but gave no news of the action. If I get any letters from any of the boys I will forward them to you.

Much love,
KIFFIN.

To Mrs. Alice Weeks
Monday, Oct. 11, 1915.

MY DEAR AUNT ALICE:

I was glad to receive your nice long letter yesterday and am glad you are comfortable and enjoying life as much as possible under the circumstances. I am taking things rather easily and not worrying as much as I usually do. The weather is too bad for much flying but I put in good time Saturday afternoon and yesterday morning. One other fellow and I have been flying on the same *appareil* and yesterday morning the chief pilot was well pleased and gave us a biograph to show the record of our flights. He told us to make one flight each and that if it was good he would give us each a good *appareil* and let us go up to our hour of two thousand meters in the afternoon. My friend started up first and had the misfortune to be caught by a strong puff of wind on starting and it ended by his smashing the *appareil* and getting off lucky by not being smashed himself. So now we are waiting for it to be repaired before we make that one flight each. But I have learned just to take things easy. Whatever flying I do from now on is part of the *épreuve* for the *brevet militaire.* In other words, I am a regular aviator now.

I get up every morning at daybreak and go out on the field and stay around watching the work and flights until seven o'clock. Then if I see I am not going to fly, I go down to the canteen with a few others and we have hot chocolate, eggs and toast and the morning paper, and spend the rest of the morning there. If I don't fly in the afternoon I go down and have tea.

No, I have not heard from Pechkoff, but Paul wrote that he had sent his regards to me. Pavelka and two other boys wrote me on the 23rd that they were soon to go into an attack. No news since. Chapman got a card from a friend who is wounded and was on the way to a hospital, but it gave no other news.

I thought I had written you how glad I was to receive the pictures. My memory seems not to be as good as it used to be and sometimes I don't know what I have or have not done. That is the truth. For the last few months it has been hard for me to concentrate my mind on anything or to think clearly. For that reason I find more trouble in writing letters than anything else. Many times I have started letters and just had to give up. When I was first here I hardly knew where I was *at.* You see, I had never been in an aëroplane before and I knew absolutely nothing about a motor. The only time I have ever been up as a passenger was the first day here, and for only about five minutes then. Yet I have been gaining as rapidly as any one and more than some. Now when I get up high I have a feeling of perfect confidence and enjoy the coming down very much. It is a great sensation. But I will tell you the truth, there were times, when I went up on an old worn-out *appareil,* that I felt as if it would be my last flight, or last of anything.

You spoke of sending me socks—I must admit that they will be very useful and I'll appreciate them. I have no warm clothes worth mentioning, but I have been counting on going to Paris most any time, when I can begin to get a supply. Warm clothes are necessary in this work.

I am glad you are learning French. I also am trying to learn and we will have to practise on each other.

Well, I think this quite a long letter to-day but had better close it now.

Much love,
KIFFIN.

Élève Pilote, École M. F.,
Camp d'Avord (Cher),
Tuesday, Oct. 12, 1915.

DEAR PAUL:

I have been glad to get your letter, enclosing the clipping about Kelly and Thorin's letter, also the money. I have heard nothing more since writing last. I wrote to Thorin and to Skipper. As there is still very heavy fighting down there, the boys left have probably had some more of it. The sergeant Skipper spoke of was of Belgian birth, but had served in the American Navy. I forget his name and it doesn't make much difference. He had been in the Legion for nine years and to me was the poorest specimen of manhood I ever met, although he always tried to curry favor with Trinkard and me. Trinkard is all right, and we can help him out a little, but there is no need of doing too much for him, as he isn't a great specimen of manhood, having very little brains.

The fellow Chapman heard from is a South American but has an American name—Preston Ames. That is all I know of him; he was in the Mitrailleuse with Chapman.

Here it goes quietly. I was just figuring up. Out of the last three weeks I have fourteen days that I haven't been in an *appareil* and most of the other seven it was only in odd minutes. Altogether, I have between twelve and fourteen hours (not sure exactly) of actual work in the five weeks I have been here. Yet when I do go up I shoot right up into the air anywhere from 1,000 to 2,000 meters high and I make fancy descents, showing perfect control of my *appareil*. Saturday morning, the last time I have flown, I was up to 2,000 meters and came down in what is known as the "spiral," or regular corkscrew descent, around and around. I was deaf for an hour afterwards, as it is hard on the ear drums. I spent all yesterday at Bourges, as it was raining here.

Love,
Kiffin.

Camp d'Avord,
Thursday, Oct. 14, 1915.

Dear Paul:

Am enclosing the letter I received from Skipper this morning. That is all the news I have received so far. You look after the wants of the boy, and then we ought again to try and get him changed.

Musgrave seems to have a charmed life, staying through all he has. If one shell killed five Americans, there must not be any left from the 2eme except Casey.

Love,
Kiffin.

To Mrs. Weeks

Thursday, Oct. 14, 1915.

Dear Aunt Alice:

I received your letter day before yesterday and the package of socks yesterday. I enjoyed your letter very much and thank you for the socks as they are very good and warm.

I received a letter from Pavelka, written Oct. 5th, but he gave little news, only said that he was still alright but that he was going back to the trenches that night. Said that owing to the fact that they were in territory formerly held by the Germans there was nothing to

83

be bought.

Tell Paul that Chapman had a letter last night saying that an American named Farnsworth was killed in a recent attack, but the letter gave no particulars. Also I got a card from Thorin in Hôpital Auxiliaire No. 20, Brau. He says he is getting along finely but he has been moved around quite a lot.

I am doing little of interest here and at times it grows very monotonous and gets on my nerves. I have been waiting for two weeks to do my finishing flights but there is always something to interfere—rain, wind, motor not working, or something. So I go to Avord or Bourges, or maybe sleep or read, and once in a while I go out to the field and fly a few minutes. When I do fly now, I go just as high up as I have the time. If I have the *appareil* for half an hour I climb 1,500 or 2,000 meters and then practise fancy descents. At times the scenery is wonderful and I will never forget the beauty of the clouds one day last week, when I was up above them. Well, if I don't finish my flights soon I am going to Paris

Much love,

KIFFIN.

Café du Commerce,
Vierzon (Cher),
Oct. 16, 1915.

DEAR PAUL:

I have time to write a few lines, although I am having the greatest time of my life. I acted foolishly yesterday but had more or less luck. I left Camp d'Avord at 2:30 o'clock for Châteauroux. It was cloudy and a little foggy, but the clouds were 800 meters high, so I started out at 600 meters, but had only gone for ten minutes when I ran into clouds only 300 or 400 meters high, so I went still higher above them all, and flew by my compass and watch.

When I thought I was near Châteauroux, I shot down through the clouds, and sure enough, I was there. I landed, and found one of the other fellows there who had broken his machine on descending. He wanted me to stay there because it was too foggy to continue, but I said that if I had found Châteauroux it was still easier to find Romorantin, so I started out again.

84

I soon ran into a heavy fog and also a little wind, so I was completely lost. For two hours I hunted for Romorantin, but could not see a d——d thing. Finally, I descended and found that I was within fifteen kilometers of Romorantin. It was nearly night, but I figured I could arrive there in ten minutes, so I asked the direction and started out again. I could not see a thing, and passed a little to the right of Romorantin without seeing it, so I was lost again. I flew for a half hour in the night and fog. I knew I was nearly out of oil and *essence,* so when I saw the lights of this town, I headed for it.

I made three turns above the town, just above the houses, trying to find a place to land, and hoping someone would have sense enough to signal to me or put out a light, but nothing happened, so finally I trusted to luck and shot down. I made a perfect landing without breaking a thing, something that would not happen one time out of a hundred under similar conditions.

Well, to end up, everyone in the town heard me and turned out to see me. To-day has been foggy so I have stayed here, and may leave to-morrow. I demanded a guard for the machine, also oil and *essence,* and a cover for the motor. So now I can rest tranquil, but I have the pick of the town for everything I want. I am followed by two or three hundred people everywhere I go. My machine is covered with flowers, also names of girls. People meet me in the streets with bouquets, and in all I am *bien content.* I have not gotten drunk yet but it is not the fault of the inhabitants, as they bring out the choicest wines from their caves.

Well, I must close now, as someone is waiting for me to go to dinner. Send me some money to Avord, as I will be breveted in two days if the weather is good, and then will

Love,
KIFFIN.

October 18, 1915.

DEAR MAMMA:

I have not written because I have been having quite a lot of experience and have been busy. The middle of last week I spent most of each day flying. Last Friday, I left here for a town about one hour's distance away. It was cloudy and foggy and I was soon lost in the fog, so I went up above it, not always a wise thing to do. I flew for an hour like that when I discovered that I was right over my town. I landed, got my papers signed and left in about fifteen minutes for another town about one hour north. There was still more fog and the wind was so that my compass was no good to me. I hunted for two hours for my town without finding it, and just at nightfall descended. I found that I was within fifteen kilometers from my town, which I figured would take me ten minutes. So I started again, but passed a little to the right of the town without seeing it, owing to the dark and fog. I continued to fly in the night for half an hour and then reached Vierzon, a town of about 40,000. I made three towns over the outskirts and picked as well as possible what I considered the best place to land. So I took the chance and shot down toward the earth without seeing it —felt my way down, as you might say—until my instinct told me I was nearly down. Then I let my machine lose its speed and settled nicely on the ground without breaking a thing. I was well satisfied, as I had been in a very dangerous position. I immediately called up the *Bureau de Place* and demanded soldiers to guard my machine and also to cover it up. Then I went into the town. The fog continued and I remained there three days and nights, having the time of my life. Everybody turned out to see me and it was practically impossible for me to walk through the streets. I was loaded down with flowers and my machine covered with them bearing girls' names and nice little messages, such as *"Vive l'Aviateur Américain Engagé Volontaire pour la France." "J'adore l' Aviateur,"* etc., and I was not allowed to pay for a thing. Sunday afternoon there were about a thousand people out begging me to fly, so I went up for a little while, but the weather was too bad for me to leave. Yesterday afternoon I did the same thing. It was still foggy and bad but after I was up in the air I suddenly took the notion to come back to camp, turned my machine in this direction and followed my compass. I was lost for a while but finally found the camp and am now waiting for good weather.

I like the aviation more and more and can now do most anything I wish, but will probably ask to learn another machine before going to the front.

I expect soon to go to Paris on *permission.*

Much love,
KIFFIN.

To Mrs. Alice Weeks
Wednesday, Oct. 20, 1915.

DEAR AUNT ALICE:

Fog and clouds always! I should almost forget what the sun looks like had I not once or twice been up high enough to get a peep at it.

I suppose Paul told you about my getting lost last Friday in the fog and landing at Vierzon in the night—quite a foolish thing. I remained three days and had a wonderful time, giving an exhibition Sunday P.M., but it was too foggy to come back to camp. Monday p.m., I went up again. It was bad weather and I couldn't see a thing, but while up I took a notion to take a chance on finding the camp and turned this way. I arrived here safely but am a little sorry that I left Vierzon, as there is nothing at all to do here but look at the fog, and everyone was surprised to see me come in when I did.

When I told my experience to the chief pilot he laughed and said it was good training for me before going to the front but that I was an old fool and lucky not to have broken my neck. It was very foolish but at the same time it has given me much confidence, and confidence is the greatest asset in this game.

I have a letter from Pavelka, written just on his arrival with the 170th Regiment, so too early for him to tell if he would be better off than in the Legion.

Hope you are nicely fixed in the new apartment but as neither you nor Paul have written me the address I will send this to the old one.

Post Card from Chartres

Oct. 21, 1915

Well, I am now a full-fledged *amateur,* ready to go to the front, if I was going on the M. Farman. The weather has been bad but I have been flying in spite of it. You had better hurry and send me

87

your new address, so I will know where to go on arrival in Paris.

Love,

KIFFIN.

To the Vicomte du Peloux
Chartres, Oct. 21, 1915.

DEAR SIR:

I arrived here this afternoon at four o'clock, leaving Avord at two. This is the finishing touch of my *épreuve* for the *brevet militaire*. Hope to be in Paris in two or three days, if the weather permits my returning to Avord in the

Sincerely,

KIFFIN.

Pilote Amateur, École Nieuport,
Camp d'Avord (Cher),
Sunday, Oct. 29, 1915.

DEAR PAUL:

I was glad to get your and Mamma's letters yesterday. There is not much news for me to write. We have been having a storm of wind and rain the last few days that has knocked the school out quite a lot. Friday night, about one o'clock, everyone was roused up to go out and try to keep the whole camp from being destroyed. The wind was blowing down the hangars, and aëroplanes were flying around all over the camp. We had about fifteen machines completely destroyed and I understand Chartres had twenty, so it has been rather expensive for the Government.

I get awfully bored here, and am sick and tired of the rear. I almost regret that I didn't go to Serbia on the Maurice Farman. But in the long run it is best for me to stay, because when I do go to the front I will be practically able to do as I please and also do some very good work.

I received a note from Skipper, written the 9th, saying that he was going that night to the trenches with extra cartouches and food and a musette full of grenades, which means another scrap. I am afraid the Boche will get him yet. It was Gache, the fellow from the Argentine, that was killed on the 29th. I hated to hear of it, because I never met a finer fellow in my life.

If we can only have a little good weather I will not waste much time here, as I intend to go just as fast as I can possibly get them to let me.

Much love,

KIFFIN.

Paris, Oct. 31, 1915

DEAR MAMMA:

I have been up here on eight days' *permission,* after finishing my *épreuve* for the *brevet militaire.* I have been here with Mrs. Weeks and Paul having a good time and trying to get fixed up for the winter. Paul is very busy and I have been much with Mrs. Weeks. She has about given up hopes of Kenneth but is very brave and I think a lot of her. I am going back to the camp to-night to begin learning a new machine. If I get the one I shall ask for I will be capable of flying any machine after learning it. When I finished my *brevet militaire* the chief pilot and the monitor recommended that I be given the very best machine to go to the front on, saying that I was a very good pilot.

You asked about finances. While in the rear studying aviation I get little pay and my expenses are heavy; but when I get to the front I will be better paid, but will have to buy most of my clothes. In flying, it is necessary to be in good condition, physically and mentally. It is cold up in the air and as I have already flown three and one half hours in one afternoon I find it necessary to get the warmest clothes possible.

What we are all doing over here is to help one another along as much as possible and, if necessary, give everything towards the final outcome. There are boys in the trenches who have now been fighting for over a year, who have nothing, and whose hardships are great. So we all try to share a little with them and some of your money has gone to give them a little more interest in life, but I hope you will not regret it. Some day the war will end with us victorious and then you will be glad of what we have done. If we should not be victorious there would be no interest left in anything to me. So I want to stake all on it.

Mrs. Weeks has made this like home to me and is now sitting near me, doing some work on my uniform.

I am sorry that I can't see you and Agnes here but we have all agreed that it would be very unwise for you to come over.

Much love,
KIFFIN.

To Mrs. Alice Weeks
Friday, Nov. 2, 1915.

DEAR MOTHER ALICE:

Well, I arrived here all o. k. yesterday morning but I found the camp rather upset. The Captain had been "fired" and sent to the front and a new captain had come to command the school. He is completely changing everything and it will be some time before things run smoothly. He is very strict and most of the men are greatly dissatisfied. When I heard all this I was rather discouraged and made up my mind to try and leave as soon as possible.

I learned that they had been asking for volunteers to go to Serbia. They are very hard to get, owing to the danger, in spite of the fact that France is paying the aviators who go there the highest salary paid by any nation. A corporal-aviator who goes to Serbia, is paid about six hundred francs a month instead of around one hundred, as on this front.

Well, yesterday I tried to see the Captain but couldn't, so I didn't do anything till this afternoon when I saw him. I expected a rough greeting, but instead he greeted me "overly nicely" and asked me what I wished. I told him that if France needed volunteers to go to Serbia I was ready to go at once on the Maurice Farman. It took him right "off his feet," and he gave me one compliment after another, telling me how proud he was to see an American volunteer for France, and one who would make such an offer. He concluded by telling me that unless I absolutely wanted to go to Serbia he preferred that I stay on this front and that I could have any *appareil* that I wished. So I asked for the Nieuport and he immediately gave it to me. How is that for diplomacy? When I left he shook hands and said several nice things which made me feel very good. We are all susceptible to flattery.   But I had something still more pleasant to come.

When I left there I went to the bureau of my old school to sign a few papers, etc. While there, the clerk, who is a friend of mine and speaks English, showed me the report that was going in about me on my papers. There was never a better report sent in on an aviator. There was a whole page of nice things of my ability as a pilot, and started off about my being an American volunteer. I can't remember all the nice things said, but a few were that I was most courageous and audacious, but at the same time prudent (that is as good as one can be), quick to learn, an intelligent, perfect pilot, and would be most invaluable at the front. I hope you will not think me too conceited, but it does make me feel good. I have done my best ever since I have been in France, but this is the first time I have felt that the military people realized it and appreciated it.

I have a mighty good start now and will try to keep it up. The new Captain's name is Boucher. If you meet anyone who knows him, it will not hurt if you let him know I am all right socially, as well as as a soldier.

Tell Paul the news and that I will write him soon.

Much love,
KIFFIN.

Pilote Aviateur, École Nieuport,
Camp d'Avord (Cher),
Saturday, Nov. 6, 1915.

DEAR PAUL:

I was glad to get your letter yesterday. I had figured out when I didn't see you at the station that you had not been able to get away soon enough. I am getting back to doing nothing here. I have spent exactly ten minutes in a machine since my return. The trouble has been rain and heavy wind. If it keeps up this way I will regret that I didn't go to the front on the Maurice Farman. But when I do finish here I will be on the best fighting machine that France has and will be able to fly any machine made, so it is worth staying for.

In order to get to the Nieuport, I have to pass on a lot of machines, but only for a short time on each. I want to spend about one half an hour on the Morane roller (that is, rolling on the ground), then about the same time on the Blériot roller, then on the Blériot 50 h.p. tour of the track, then B.—60 h.p., the B.—80 h.p., then Morane 50 h.p., 60 h.p., and 80 h.p., then Morane Parasol, and afterward I will pass on to the Nieuport. Of course on each it only means a very short time but it is nearly always bad weather now and a lot of people on each machine. I don't do a bit of work now, not even to help fill the motor or move the machine about.

The new captain has changed things about quite a lot, trying to put a little system and *militaire* in the school, but the men object to it and are causing trouble. Night before last they tried to make an *appel* of the works at nine o'clock. But the men made a rough-house of it, putting out all the lights and yelling at the top of their voices. As a result, the whole place is under a kind of *consigne* for two weeks, and no one will be given permission to go to Bourges or anywhere.

Give Bob S. [Soubiran] my regards. I would like to have him with me, but if it is worked it will have to be done from Paris. The thing to do is to state that Bob is an expert mechanic and that as such he wants to go in the aviation, and that he wants to go to the front as my mechanic, we both being Americans and friends and my having absolute confidence in his ability.

Will close now, as I hope to do a little rolling this afternoon.

Much love,
KIFFIN.

To the Vicomte du Peloux
Avord, Nov. 10, 1915.

MY DEAR FRIEND:

I have been intending writing ever since I came back, but have little news.

When I got back I found that we had a new captain in charge of the school. He has made a number of changes and the school is more strict than before. Most of the men have been a little dissatisfied but he is very nice to me and I don't mind a little system to the school.

I am now preparing for the Nieuport but before learning to fly it I must be able to pilot the different Blériots and Moranes. I have only been in a machine four times, about ten minutes each time, since coming back; but am learning very quickly for what time I do spend at it.

Regards to your wife.

Sincerely yours,

KIFFIN.

Camp d'Avord, Thursday, Nov. 18, 1915.

DEAR PAUL:

I was glad to get your letter and the letters from home yesterday. I have been expecting any day to leave here, but it seems I will be longer than I thought. I went to the Captain to-day and asked him to send me to Le Bourget, but he told me that he cannot do it. He has the order not to send any more pilots there right now, and is waiting for further orders. They have been talking of changing the General Reserve, and I am afraid that is what is being done now, which will mean that I will not be in Paris.

They are expecting an instructor for the Nieuport now, so as soon as the weather permits I will probably start to flying it. Lately I have been doing as I please. I get up when I feel like it and go up to the camp, and if I want to fly a little around the country, I tell the mechanicians to prepare my Morane Parasol, which no one uses but me, perhaps take a passenger with me and go out for half an hour or an hour, then come back home and sleep, or do as I like. Sometimes, I go up and do a few acrobatic stunts.

But all in all, I have only flown about ten hours since being back here. Yesterday, I tried going up in a very strong wind. My machine was doing all kind of fancy tricks with me so I didn't stay long. I landed all right but was bringing my machine into the hangars when the wind blew it clear over sideways. Broke it a little, but only required an hour or so's work by the mechanics to make the repairs. To-day, I went up in the rain, and stayed twenty minutes in the clouds.

Hope everything is going well with you.

Much love,

KIFFIN.

93

To the Vicomte du Peloux

Avord, Nov. 22, 1915.

MY DEAR FRIEND:

I was very glad to receive your letter a few days ago. We had bad weather till five days ago and since then it is cold. But I take advantage of all weather that will do and have learned first to pilot the Blériots and then went on the Morane. We have three or four Nieuports here but no one flies them. They said something to-day about some of us trying the Nieuport, but I prefer to wait till I go to Le Bourget, where the Nieuport is understood.

I expect to go to Le Bourget most any time now. The only drawback is that they say I have learned too fast and have not enough hours of flight. The Morane is supposed to be the hardest machine to learn to pilot, and after learning it one is supposed to be able to learn to pilot any of them. Yet, so far, I have found it the easiest thing I have ever done. I do anything I want to on it in a practically perfect manner. If I do happen to break a machine now they can't say that it is because I do not know how to manage it. I suppose I am a little conceited but everyone here regards me as *un as,* and I am satisfied, as I like to succeed at whatever I undertake. But of course the way to prove it will be when I am at the front, which I await with impatience.

I have a special *permission* which entitles me to do as I please. So I have a room out from the camp and am really very comfortable.

My kindest regards to your wife.

Sincerely,

KIFFIN.

Pilote-Aviateur,
École Nieuport,
Camp d'Avord,
Monday, Nov. 22, 1915.

DEAR PAUL:

I was glad to receive your card yesterday and to know that everything was going well with you. To-day has been foggy and bad and I have done nothing. But until to-day we have had five days of fairly good weather and I have made good use of those five days. I have gone faster than I ever dreamed of going. I finished all the

Blériots and have gotten complete control of the Morane. I am now ready to go to Le Bourget most any day. The only thing is I have gone so fast that they don't want me to leave yet. They say that I ought to have more hours of flight. Most men take from six weeks to three months to do what I have done since being back here. I don't know, but it just seemed to come naturally to me and I have always had absolute confidence and so have been able to do anything I have wanted to.

They have three or four Nieuports here, but no one flies on them. They may want me to fly on one of them but I had rather wait until I go to Le Bourget, where they know something about it. Then I am beginning to think of asking for a machine that I never dreamed of asking for before. It is the Morane Monacock. There are only a few men who fly it at the front and they are known as the Kings of the Air. It is the same machine to pilot as the one I am now flying. The only thing is that it is used for nothing at all except to fight, and you are all alone in it and must have much sangfroid and courage. Then your machine gun is fixed so that you aim it by maneuvering the aëroplane, which is more or less difficult. The Chief Pilot told me to-day that I might demand it when I go to Le Bourget, but that he was doubtful of my being able to get it before going to the front on the Nieuport and bringing down at least one or more Aviatiks. That looks like a far-off thing, but one fellow made the remark to-day that he would give me not more than two months before I either brought one down or broke my neck. There is one other man here who has gone like me, he is the twin brother of Navarre, France's greatest living *aviateur,* who has brought down seven *Aviatiks* with the Morane Monacock. We two hope to go to Le Bourget this week, but I don't know; it depends on the higher authorities.

I suppose Mrs. Weeks has told you that I wrote about my living out for the last week, having taken a little house with Victor Chapman, where we have a cook and all. In other words, I am perfectly free from the *militaire.*

Well, this is about all, so will close.

Much love,
KIFFIN.

Monday, Nov. 22, 1915.

My dear Aunt Alice:

Letters from you have been coming more frequently lately and have kept me in good spirits, and I thank you very much for them and also for the socks which I received to-day.

The weather has been rather cold lately but I have been bundled up and not suffered much except with my hands when flying.

When I go to Paris I must try and find some kind of special glove. I was foolish not to have let you get the fur coat for me while I was there, but you can give it to me when I go back, which I hope will be very soon. It will not be necessary, however, for the extra lining. With five days of fairly good weather I have gone like a "house on fire" and yesterday I spent two hours and a half flying the Morane.

I am now thinking of going to Le Bourget most any time. I received a very nice letter from Georges de Fontenailles written from Tours. Also heard from Musgrave, who is still at the same hospital. Have heard nothing from Pavelka and am afraid for the boy's welfare. Believe me, dear, I feel that I have many scores to settle, and there is going to be more than one "Boche" aviator to settle them, or I will not live to tell the tale. As the French say, I am *vraiment un as* when in the air, and I am going to take advantage of if. Have several letters to write, so will close.

Much love,
KIFFIN.

Nov. 26, 1915.

Dear Mamma:

A card from Paul says he is forwarding some letters from you which I shall be glad to get, as I haven't heard for some little time.

Am ready to leave the camp and will go to the General Reserve as soon as they ask for more men which will be within a week or two. The General Reserve is right out of Paris and I shall be glad to get there, as I expect to ask permission to stay in Paris most of the time.

I now rank as one of the best pilots and am considered as capable of flying any aëroplane. I think nothing of doing things in the air that men were paid thousands of dollars to do before the war. I do them that I may be prepared to put my machine in any position I want to when at the front and to be able to meet any emergency. I shall fly the fastest and best machine France has and naturally will be given important work. I am giving the best that is in me in this war and will not stop at anything as long as it helps toward the final victory. This is a war of *the world* and means as much to the people of America as it does to anyone else. There is not one human being who is not being affected by the war. So no one has the right to forget about it or lose interest in it.

To-day is one of the coldest days I ever felt in France. I went up for fifteen minutes this morning and when I came down my hands were almost frozen in spite of my gloves.

Much love,
KIFFIN.

Dec. 3, 1915.

DEAR MAMMA:

Well, I am still here at Camp d'Avord, flying a little when the weather permits, which is not often. I have been expecting to leave here for some time but now will probably be here a week or more longer. I have all the liberty here I could want. Have my own machine, which no one uses but me, and only fly whenever I want to.

However, I am usually in the air when the weather is half-way good. To-day it rained until about 3 P.M. and then stopped. I immediately went out, as it was the finest time for three days, and stayed out till dark.

I have piloted three different makes of machines and now am supposed to be able to pilot any of them, so expect to nearly always have my choice of the different machines. My promotion naturally will depend more or less on what I do at the front. In France, the aviators start in as simple soldiers, unless their rank is higher beforehand. I have been made corporal, and when I get to the front should be made sergeant.

Much love,
KIFFIN.

Dec. 14, 1915.

DEAR MAMMA:

I am now at the General Reserve of the Aviation, getting a little more entrainment on the Nieuport and waiting to be assigned to an escadrille at the front. This is right out of Paris and I spend most of the time there, as the weather is nearly always bad, and then I sleep there every night. I find Paul and Mrs. Weeks and, in fact, everyone well and in good spirits.

I had dinner one night last week with Monsieur du Peloux and have chances to go out to dinner very often, but I try not to accept many invitations, as I like plenty of sleep now.

I am expecting to spend all this month here, so will have a good Christmas dinner that Mrs. Weeks is planning. I hope that you will have a good Christmas and that if Agnes goes to Grandma's, you will go too.

Much love,
KIFFIN.

Jan. 7, 1916.

DEAR MAMMA:

I am still here, just outside of Paris. The weather is nearly always bad, so it means little activity in the aviation and less demand for more pilots for the front. I am still taking things very easy. When we do have a day fairly good I fly a little and the rest of the time I stay in Paris. I seldom go around, however, in Paris and dread it every time I have an invitation out to dinner. Paul, Mrs. Weeks and I stay very quietly at home and I usually go off to bed as soon as we have finished dinner.

New Year's night, Paul and I dined with our good friends the du Peloux, and that is about the extent of my doings since I wrote last.

I hope you are taking a good rest and feeling much better by now.

Much love,
KIFFIN.

LETTERS FROM THE AVIATION

General Reserve,
Jan. 17, 1916.

DEAR MAMMA:

I am still here and as I am now starting to fly still another machine, a new Nieuport, I shall be here at least two weeks longer. It is still cold and bad weather, and little doing. We have just had news that Kenneth Weeks and the other boys reported missing on June 16th last were killed. Mrs. Weeks had really had stronger hopes than any of us concerning them. It is very sad for us all. Mrs. Weeks is brave and her interest now is in doing all she can for the ones of us who are left.

Everyone seems hopeful of the final outcome. When Bulgaria went in there was a feeling of unrest and also the political change upset people a little, but now there is optimism. The more the people go through, the stronger and more determined they become.

Much love,
KIFFIN.

Plessis-Belleville,
Division Nieuport, G. D. E. Secteur 92A,
Tuesday.

MY DEAR AUNT ALICE:

We are all settled here, Thaw, Chapman and I climbed into the "1st class wagon" yesterday morning and had a nice trip up, taking about an hour. When we arrived we were the first off the train and hurried over to the only hotel here, which is only about two hundred yards from the Division. We found four rooms and took them all, as Prince was to come this morning. We also made an arrangement for our meals here, and it is not so very expensive, considering everything. It is a rather God-forsaken country, but could be worse. I was rather lonesome last night. We had a fire in one of the rooms and sat around and read until ten o'clock. This morning at seven, Thaw's orderly came around and woke us all, brought up the coffee and then brushed our clothes.

I call that living in pretty good style; don't you?

There was no flying this morning, so we took a rifle and went hunting but didn't kill anything.   We did get up a very good appetite for lunch, which we have just finished.

They say that no *permissions* are given from here to Paris, but will run in once in a while. Will write you often to let you know that I am always all right and thinking of you.

Much love,
KIFFIN.

Plessis-Belleville,
February 17, 1916.

DEAR MAMMA:

Still little news. The weather has been very bad for the last two weeks, and practically nothing at all doing for the aviators. However, they are organizing the American Escadrille, and everything is all right, so we may leave soon. In all probability will go to Belfort. It is a very beautiful country around there, and I imagine will be rather interesting.

Now, I do not want you to worry about me. If I die, I want you to know that I have died as every man ought to die fighting for what is right. I do not feel that I am fighting for France alone, but for the cause of all humanity, the greatest of all causes.

Here where I am, I read and sleep most of the time. I go in to Paris every two or three days for the night to see Paul. I have been feeling fairly well, but impatient at the inaction. There are a lot of people now a little under the weather with la grippe, the same as you have been having in America. I was in Paris night before last, and found that Paul was feeling it a little, but suppose he is all right now. Hope you are still improving in health.

With much love,
KIFFIN.

Paris, March 11, 1916.

DEAR MAMMA:

We are still having bad weather, snowing every day, and seldom any flying can be done. I have been feeling fairly well, except for a little cold.

The fighting at Verdun is as heavy as ever, but we now seem to be holding. I've been rather expecting and hoping to go down there,

100

but, so far, "nothing doing."

I came into Paris to-day and am not going out for a couple of days, so may have orders when I get out there.

I thought it rather amusing when I read yesterday about Villa going over and taking Columbus, N. M. Suppose the Germans are backing him, hoping to keep the U. S. busy there.

From now on mail may be rather uncertain, owing to the renewed activity of the submarines. Have just noticed some change in the mail schedule for America.

Much love,
KIFFIN.

To the Vicomte du Peloux
Plessis-Belleville,
April 6, 1916.

MY DEAR FRIEND:

I suppose you have been wondering why I have not written before this, but I really have not had anything to write.

The fact is I have been more or less demoralized by never doing anything and waiting each day to go to the front. I ask each week to be attached to a regular French escadrille, but they continue to keep us all back, waiting until the Escadrille Américaine is formed. Why they don't form it, I don't know. We have enough men ready, the material ready, know who will be the captain, that we are to go to Belfort, and that our number is "N. 124." Yet we are not sent out. In the meantime, I fly a little and spend much time in Paris.

I have now written a captain at Verdun to please ask for me to be attached to his escadrille if he has a vacancy. I hope you and your wife are having a pleasant stay in the South.

Kindest regards to you both.

Sincerely,
KIFFIN.

Escadrille N. 124,
Luxeuil-les-Bains,
April 20, 1916.

DEAR MAMMA:

I am at last in escadrille but a good distance from the front and, so far, it is like being on a pleasant trip to a resort. This is a resort in time of peace with the hot baths and hot water to drink coming up out of the ground.

We are just forming the American escadrille and it will be nearly a month before we really get down to work. Our captain is a young fellow and one of us. We all eat together at an hotel where wonderfully good meals are served. We occupy a villa that has been requisitioned for us, with orderlies to wait on us. We go down each day about one hundred yards from here to bathe in a bath-house that is over two hundred years old. The scenery around the town is wonderful and we ride over the surrounding country with our captain and are planning to do a little fishing and hunting, so you can see that it is not much like being at war. But we may not stay long, and if we do, we will have some good work to do when everything is ready. We are under the orders of the most famous man in the French aviation—not for bringing down Germans but for going over into Germany—and we are to be guards for his outfit. He is a man absolutely without fear and one of the most interesting characters I ever met. He always goes at the head of his men and the Germans have quite a prize on his head. So with him we will be able to do some very good work. I shall like to go with him a few times, but not to finish the war under him.

I am sitting by my window now with a good warm sun coming in and a wonderful view and the birds singing. If it were not for looking in the glass and seeing myself in uniform I should not be able to believe that I am at war, or that there is such a thing as war.

My love to everybody.

Much love,
KIFFIN.

LETTERS FROM THE AVIATION

Escadrille N. 124,
Luxeuil-les-Bains,
Thursday, April 20, 1916.

DEAR PAUL:

I just wrote Mrs. Weeks a long letter and if you don't mind, let it kind of do for both of you, as it is hard for me to write two long letters the same day. Going to Rosenay was a mistake, but interesting to me, as I rode in an auto over a great deal of the road we went over on our famous 56-kilometer march, and also over the road from Epernay towards Reims.

Near Rosenay I passed a detachment of the Legion, but didn't know it until we had gone by them, so didn't get to talk to them. I spent Tuesday night in Epernay; in going in passed the town of Hauteville, where we slept that night and had the big bonfire out in the courtyard of the church, or whatever it was.

I think that we will only stay here about a month to get really organized, when we will probably change sectors to more action. If we had plenty of work to do here this would be the dream of the war, with our villa to live in, thermal baths, and a good hotel to eat at.

Last night, the Captain showed us some wonderful photographs that he has. I will be able to make a collection of fine ones. The Captain is going to try to get for each of us a photograph that is amazing. It is actually a picture of a Voisin in air, falling in flames with the Fokker close to it, taken by a third aëroplane arriving too late to save the Voisin. The man who took the picture was killed the following morning by the same Fokker, and the day after his best friend killed the man in the Fokker.

Well, the boys are hollering for me, so, as I said before, I hope you won't mind letting my letter to Mrs. Weeks kind of do for both of you. I will always keep one or the other of you posted on all I am doing.

Much love,
KIFFIN.

Postcard from Luxeuil, post-marked April 25, 1916
Glad to receive your letter to-day. Nothing to do here, no machines; everything seems awfully slow. I wrote yesterday about

your coming here. Think you would like it for a few weeks.

Love,

KIFFIN.

Escadrille N. 124,
Luxeuil-les-Bains,
Saturday (April 29, 1916).

DEAR PAUL:

I was glad to get your letter night before last and hope that you will come on down. A little vacation won't hurt you, and then you might write something while here, and talking to all the boys would interest you.

We still have no machines, and the Germans continue to show up—three more yesterday. Great big slow things; one good man with a *Bébé* could have gotten all three of them before they could have gotten back to their lines.

Thaw and Hall have just showed up. Day before yesterday I went to Gerardmer, about two hours ride from here to the funeral of a pilot to whom the doctors gave too much chloroform for a minor operation and killed. Had lunch with the officers of an Escadrille near here. One of the best lunches I ever had, as that is recognized as one of the best *popotes* on the front. Yesterday, we had the funeral of our driver who was killed. Funerals are great affairs, as aviators come to them from all over the surrounding country.

If that Committee ever comes to amount to anything it may be useful.

Thénault said he couldn't propose us for sergeants until we got to work, but would do so the first week of flying. I have twinges of rheumatism again, but the baths here may do it good, and it will not interfere with my work. The people here are all very nice to us.

Love,

KIFFIN.

Luxeuil,
Sunday, April 30, 1916.

MY DEAR AUNT ALICE:

The last two days have been rainy, but in spite of that I had

104

a wonderful trip yesterday. We all piled into the Captain's car yesterday morning at seven to take a tour of the country between here and the lines, to see the few places where it is possible to land, and to visit the other escadrilles.

The scenery is marvelous and I never had such a trip before, in spite of the rain and the cold in some of the mountains. We went to Belfort and from there northeast. I made my first trip into Germany as we went through the section of Alsace that we hold, passing in some places within a couple of kilometers of the Germans. The prettiest scenery of all was looking down on Thann and the valley surrounding it. We went down through the town and the valley; then in cutting back through the mountains the road wound around like a snake and we could look down and behold the most magnificent scenery. We didn't get home till 7 P.M. and all of us were rather tired, and after a good dinner went to bed.

I have been stirring around this A.M. for some time and have had breakfast, but the others are only now beginning to get up.

Thaw and Cowden are still in Paris, but have telegraphed that they and Hall would be here to-morrow. It makes but little difference, as we have no machines so far. This is not in the war-zone and is a nice quiet place with the baths and water I have already told you about. Living is not expensive and I think you and Paul would enjoy it here and get benefit. Of course I shall be busy but I'd like to know you both were here.

Much love,
KIFFIN.

To the Vicomte et Vicomtesse du Peloux
Escadrille, N. 124, Luxeuil-les-Bains,
May 1, 1916.

MY DEAR FRIENDS:

I was very glad to get your letter, forwarded from Plessis. I left there two weeks ago to-day, but am not yet at work, as our machines have not yet arrived, which you can guess makes me very impatient. However, this is a nice country, beautiful scenery, healthy climate, and very sympathetic people. Since being here I have spent much time riding over the surrounding country in auto, and have seen

105

some very wonderful scenery and enjoyed it very much. One day, I was over in Alsace, through the Thann Valley, and back across the mountains. Another day, I was at Gerardmer and came back through the Val d'Ajol (not sure of spelling). So you can see, I am a little better than being at Plessis.

I get rather angry some mornings when the Germans come over here and I can't do anything. If we only had our machines, certainly we could have brought down some of them, as they have such a long way to go to get back to their lines.

With kindest regards to you both,

Sincerely,
KIFFIN.

Jim is here also.

Luxeuil-les-Bains
Saturday (May 6, 1916).

DEAR PAUL:

Well, I am at last about to get down to work. The Captain, Lt. de Laage, Thaw, Hall and myself, have our machines, although we haven't yet arranged our mitrailleuses. I took my machine out yesterday afternoon for its first flight. When I left the field there was not a breath of wind and the air was very heavy. I flew around for awhile at only two thousand meters, then started down. Just as I got to about 700 meters, a big gale came up that lifted a Maurice Farman off the ground and dashed it to pieces. When it first struck me, I thought that my machine was going to pieces. The Captain and everyone were scared to death for me, but I kept my motor going, turned face in the wind, and just kind of dropped to the ground. I didn't think of any danger for myself, but was only afraid for my machine, as I knew I would have to wait a long time for another.

Well, I landed without breaking a thing, and then eight or ten men came running out to help me get the machine in without the wind turning it over. They all felicitated me, and I didn't regret the event, as it gives me a good start.

In regard to photographs, every single fellow seems to be trying to beat the others in sending news to the newspapers, so there is going to be a d——d sight too much publicity as it is, and every time the least thing happens, four or five will be sending telegrams to the papers. So I had rather not bother with any of it as all this junk they pull off makes me sick. The Captain has been having a photographer take different pictures, and all of us get copies of them, which I will give to you. But any picture of any interest will be in the hands of newspapers before I could get it to you. Some of us are trying to get an agreement made, that for any general pictures that are sold the money received is to go towards the expenses of the Escadrille. X. is taking some pictures in to-day, to be sold if possible for the benefit of the Escadrille. X. is always busy taking pictures of every little thing and if he can sell them, let him do so, he needs the money. I haven't taken any yet, as I thought you were coming, and could take whatever interested you, after we had gotten our machines.

I am hoping to go over the lines and try my hand out soon.

Still don't know whether to expect you or not.

Love,
KIFFIN.

Escadrille N. 124,
Luxeuil-les-Bains,
Wednesday, May 10, 1916.

DEAR PAUL:

I received your letter Sunday morning, enclosing the 50 francs, and thank you for same. I am really not in need of anything now, unless I buy some clothes. I have been wanting to buy another uniform, but I passed through Belfort to-day on my way to another Escadrille to get a machine and bring back here; at Belfort I thought I would order a uniform, but found the tailors there very ordinary, so think I will try and wait until I get to Paris again, or to some other sector.

I have not done anything special lately, but have been getting up at all hours and pretending to be busy as everything. There was really a lot of work to get everything right, and then I have had to learn the territory. I think that I am all ready now. I will take your pictures the first good day that I am not too busy, but would really prefer that you write nothing about us. Any time that one of us brings down a Boche will write you about it, but outside of that I hate to see anything at all come out about us.

Jim and Chapman now have their machines and are busy arranging them. Prince is at Paris to get his machine and bring it here. Bert and Thaw are doing the same as me. That is all I know to write.

Mrs. Weeks wrote that you were coming down. If so, you can get all the pictures you want and see what the boys have to say.

Much love,
KIFFIN.

Post Card:

DEAR PAUL:

No news, as no one is flying at present, owing to weather, Eyre was here yesterday taking pictures. I don't expect to do anything for a couple of days longer.

Love,
KIFFIN.

Telegram from Jim McConnell

Luxeuil, 18 Mai, 1916.

Kiffin a descendu un Boche. Il a tiré a trente mètres, tué mitrailleur et pilote tombé en flammes sur les tranchées boches. Médaille Militaire proposé.

JIM.

(Kiffin has brought down a Boche. He fired at thirty meters. Killed the mitrailleur and the pilot, who fell with the machine in flames into the German trenches. Has been proposed for the military medal.

JIM.)

Escadrille N. 124,
Luxeuil-les-Bains,
Thursday, May 18, 1916.

DEAR PAUL:

Well, at last I have a little news for you. This morning I went out over the lines to make a little tour. I was a little the other side of the lines, when my motor began to miss a bit. I turned around to go to a camp near the lines. Just as I started to head for there, I saw a Boche machine about seven hundred meters under me and a little inside our lines. I immediately reduced my motor, and dived for him. He saw me at the same time, and began to dive towards his lines. It was a machine with a pilot and mitrailleur, with two mitrailleuses, one facing the front and one the rear that turned on a pivot, so he (the gunner) could fire in any direction. He immediately opened fire on me and my machine was hit, but I didn't pay any attention to that and kept going straight for him, until I got within twenty-five or thirty meters of him. Then, just as I was afraid of running into him, I fired four or five shots, then swerved my machine to the right to keep from running into him. As I did that, I saw the mitrailleur fall back dead on the pilot, the mitrailleuse fall from its position and point straight up in the air, the pilot fall to one side of the machine as if he was done for also. The machine itself first fell to one side, then dived vertically towards the ground with a lot of smoke coming out of the rear. I circled around, and three or four minutes later saw a lot of smoke coming up from the ground just beyond the German trenches. I had hoped that he would fall in our lines, as it is hard to prove when they fall in the German lines. The post of observation signalled seeing the machine fall, and the smoke. The Captain said he would propose me for the Médaille Militaire, but I don't know whether I will get it or not.

Yesterday, Thaw had a fine fight with one that ended up by the Boche diving towards the ground. He was signalled as leaving the air on being seriously hit, but being able to get in his lines.

Am very busy now, as the order has just come for us to go to Verdun. Jim sent you a telegram. Percy Noel is down here and so is going to write the story of my fight. Can't be helped.

Will write you again when I get to new location. Just address Escadrille N. 124, without the sector.

Love,
KIFFIN.

Escadrille N. 124,
Monday, May 22, 1916.

DEAR PAUL:

I have only time for a line, as it is nearly supper time, and I must sleep as soon as I finish eating and get up at three A.M.

Bertie Hall attacked a Boche this afternoon at 4,000 meters high, brought him down. He followed him to one thousand meters high and saw him hit the ground and go to pieces just in the German lines. Bertie's machine was hit in the fight. I was flying at 1,500 meters high over the Fort Douaumont, protecting the observation machines during the attack. This is a regular hell around here in the way of excitement and the world going crazy. Impossible to express with words one's impressions. I am badly played out for lack of sleep. Poor Jim is still at Luxeuil; it was really not his fault. His machine was poor and broke when it shouldn't have, and he is waiting there. Will write long letter when I can.

Much love,
KIFFIN.

Give Bertie some publicity.

Escadrille N. 124,
Secteur 24,
Tuesday, May 23, 1916.

DEAR PAUL:

I wrote you a short letter yesterday but mailed it without stamps, so don't know whether it will go or not. So will write you another one, as I want you to give Bertie Hall some publicity. Yesterday morning, he dived on three Boches in their lines, didn't get any of them but was lucky they didn't get him. Yesterday afternoon, he attacked an Aviatik at four thousand meters high over our lines, killed the pilot, then as the machine was falling in the German lines, he followed it down to a thousand meters high and saw it smash up on the ground. The post of observation saw it also, so it is official.

I was guarding the observation machine at 1,500 meters high, so didn't have any fighting, although saw plenty going on on the ground. Cowdin and Prince have shown up here at last. Poor Jim is still stuck at Luxeuil through hard luck. Am sorry you and Mrs.

Weeks talked so much, as my German fell in their lines, which is not as good as falling in ours.

Love,
KIFFIN.

Verdun, May 23, 1916.

DEAR MAMMA:

I have been pretty much on the go and having some excitement for the last week, and am tired out for lack of sleep-I brought down a German machine in the German lines, but am sure I killed the two men in it. Have been feeling pretty good over it and am proposed for the Médaille Militaire and the Croix de Guerre.

The escadrille was ordered up here where the great fighting is going on and we have plenty to do to keep us busy. Words are impossible to express one's impressions here as this is the greatest thing in the history of the world. Yesterday afternoon, I flew for two hours, circling around over the "Mort Homme," at a very low altitude, protecting the observation machines. The most terrible fighting was going on underneath me the whole time. But I am not going to try to express my impressions, because I can't. At the same time I was doing that, one of my friends was over my head, about 1,500 feet high, having a death struggle with a German machine, which he succeeded in bringing down.

We are very nicely quartered here, having a very nice villa to live in, having a cook also, so that we don't have to go out for our meals. We are certainly living an incongruous life. We live like princes when not working. An auto comes and takes us up to the field; we climb into our machines (which the mechanics have taken care of), they fasten us in and fix us up snugly, and put the motor en route, and away we go for two or three hours, to prowl through the air, looking for an enemy machine to dive on and have it out with.

About a week ago, we all gave flights before a moving picture concern. The pictures are going to be shown in America. If you see them advertised be sure and go, and look for a machine with an "R."

on the side and that will be Kiffin.

A great deal of love,

KIFFIN.

Escadrille N. 124,

Secteur 24,

May 30, 1916.

DEAR MAMMA:

I suppose the papers have given you more information than I can write, but anyway, last week was rather exciting.

Last Wednesday morning, I went out and had eight fights, all of them being inside the German lines, so I couldn't tell how much damage I did. Two of the other fellows brought down one machine each, I assisting at one. Finally, I attacked a German about ten kilometers within their lines, and was following him towards the ground, when suddenly there were machines all around me shooting away and I thought for a minute or two that I was going to stay in Germany, especially when an explosive bullet came through my windshield and exploded in my face. I got four or five little pieces around my mouth, but that makes no difference, and I am most well now. But when they hit me, what with the blood and the shock, I didn't know much of what was happening. But I got back to our lines o. k. and landed where there was a field ambulance. Went to Paris for a couple of days, but am now back on the job, getting a new machine fixed up, and hope soon to be back at work.

Much love,

KIFFIN.

Escadrille N. 124,

Secteur 24,

Friday, June 2, 1916.

DEAR PAUL:

I am still waiting for my machine to be fixed up, and so am not doing anything. I certainly felt badly yesterday at noon, when I didn't have a machine. You will probably see it in the papers and know why. Tell Thaw I would have given anything if he had been here and both of us with machines, that we would certainly have

112

had the chance to bring down some Germans in our lines. The rest of the escadrille were out, but it was a series of hard luck with them. I thought I was going to be killed by the bombs, which was a very disgusting feeling; as it is, they got a great number of women and children.

In regard to the picture: that film I think is at Luxeuil, and there is no chance of ever finding it. Some pretty day I will take some pictures of all of us and send to you.

I am hoping that I at least get to work to-morrow.

Much love,

KIFFIN.

P.S. For Heaven's sake, let's try and shut down on the publicity about the Escadrille!

Escadrille N. 124,
Secteur 24,
Monday, June 5, 1916.

DEAR PAUL:

Little news. Mr. Charles Prince is here for dinner tonight, and he brought along the phonograph, which you can tell Eyre we appreciate very much.

My citation hasn't yet gone through, so can't send you a copy yet. Don't think there is much doubt of the Médaille, but don't expect two citations. There is no reason why I shouldn't have them, except that we are very unlucky in having a captain who is a nice fellow and brave, but doesn't know how to look after his men, and doesn't try to. I have been fighting with him ever since being back, mainly about the fact that I have no machine, he having given my old one to Prince and not managing right about getting me a new one. I think that in a few weeks I will be pretty sick with the outfit. I am going to try my d——dest to get another German machine down well within the French lines. Then I think things will change a little.

The Colonel's name is Barès (I think that is the way it is spelled; it is pronounced Barras). He has been the head of the Aviation since the beginning of the war.

Will keep you posted.

Love,
KIFFIN.

Escadrille N. 124,
Secteur 24,
Sunday, June 11, 1916.

DEAR PAUL:

It has been such bad weather all this week that there has been nothing doing. I finally got my new machine and have it all regulated. Did get one flight late Friday, over the lines, but nothing exciting. Saw a few Germans but it was too cloudy to do any good. The Escadrille is now pretty full, as we have been reinforced by Johnson, Lufbery, Balsley, Rumsey and Hill. The captain has also asked for Skipper and Masson a number of times, so we look for them any time.

Just saw a pilot on a Maurice Farman do a d——d stupid thing about twenty minutes ago. They have just carried the pilot and mechanician off to the hospital, and they will be lucky if they live. I feel sorry for the poor mechanician, but not for the pilot, as there is little excuse for him. He left the ground too close to the hangar, and ran full into an iron wind indicator, then went head-on into a wall.

Much love,
KIFFIN.

Escadrille N. 124,
Secteur 24,
Saturday, June 17, 1916.

DEAR PAUL:

Well, the last two days have seen a lot of action in the air, but none of us has had much luck. I myself was caught twice yesterday by surprise, when I was watching for it at the same time, and being very careful in what I was doing. The only reason that I didn't get brought down was that the Boche shot poorly. I was attacking machines all the time, but they were always too many.

Chapman has been a little too courageous and got me into one of the mess-ups because I couldn't stand back and see him get it

114

alone. He was attacking all the time, without paying much attention. He did the same thing this morning, and wouldn't come home when the rest of us did. The result was that he attacked one German, when a Fokker which we think was Boelke (the papers say he was killed but we don't believe it), got full on Chapman's back, shot his machine to pieces and wounded Chapman in the head. It is just a scratch but a miracle that he wasn't killed. Part of the commands on Chapman's machine were broken, but Chapman landed by holding them together with his hand.

The Germans came over yesterday afternoon and to-day and bombarded us. I didn't see them yesterday. To-day, I went up, but my motor didn't work. When I left the ground, one of the bougies broke, so I was unable to get to their height. There were four machines whose motors didn't work, because we had been doing too much flying beforehand. The others had fights with the Germans, but none were brought down, so the Escadrille is not in overly good favor and the newspapers speaking of us in a praising manner don't sound overly good.

Navarre was wounded to-day. Then I saw a pilot and his passenger killed and burned up in a machine, but that was the fault of the pilot.

I had thought beforehand that yesterday and to-day I would try my d——dest to kill one or two Germans for the boys who got it this time last year, but as I say had no luck. Am tired out now. Have been out four different times to-day, and all the while going up and down. One time I dropped straight down from 4,050 meters to 1,800 meters on top of a Boche, but he got away. It tires you out a lot, the change in heights and maneuvering.

Will close now.

Love,
KIFFIN.

Escadrille N. 124,
Monday, June 19, 1916.

DEAR PAUL:

Well, yesterday was a rather bad day for us. You know we didn't think much of Balsley. It was because he is young and inexperienced, but when he got here to the Escadrille I began to like him fairly well and better every day, as I saw he had plenty of good will to work and was not afraid. Well, yesterday, we all left for an offensive barrage over the lines. We were all supposed to follow the Captain, but only Prince, Balsley and myself did so. We four were over the lines, when we ran across about forty Boches in one little sector, flying at different heights. At the top, where we were, there were twelve or fifteen little *"Aviatiks de Chasse,"* which go just as fast as we do, and in addition they carry a passenger. The pilot shoots like we do, but has a man to the rear of him who has a second gun that can cover the rear and sides. We were only four and over the German lines, but we stayed close together and for ten or fifteen minutes circled around the Boches, they shooting at us nearly all the time from four or five hundred meters.

Finally, we saw our chance. One of their machines crossed over between us and our lines, while all the others were in the rear of us. We immediately went down on this one Boche, which of course caused a general mix-up, as Boches came from the sides and rear. I saw either Prince or Balsley go over in a regular death drop and thought to myself that he was killed. Then I lost sight of the other one, and only the captain and I were left, so we got out of it and finally came home, thinking the other two were killed. Prince came home soon afterwards, having had to drop straight down, owing to a Boche having the upper hand on him and putting a bullet through his casque, but not wounding him.

Poor Balsley seems to have dived on one Boche, gotten close to him, and when he tried to shoot, his gun fired one shot, then jammed. He turned off, and as he did a bullet caught him in the hip, and exploded on hitting the bone. He fell straight down but luckily had his feet strapped to the commands, and was able to readdress the machine and land with one foot. He just landed inside our lines, and really had a hell of a close call, and his machine was completely smashed on landing.

At present we are not sure of his wound. It may turn out to be only a slight thing, but several pilots have died from being wounded like that, getting blood poison. Then they can't tell yet if any of the bullet went into his stomach or not. All this is not for the press, it is just to let you know. If you give out anything only say that Balsley was slightly wounded in fighting against several machines, and that he has been proposed for the Médaille Militaire for bravery. I understand that his mother is very poor, and was dependent on him to run their bakery business, when he left and came over here, and that now the family is in very hard lines.

Chapman is all right; only a scratch, and will be flying to-morrow, having received a new and better machine. Unofficially, Thaw receives the Legion and me the Médaille, but the papers have not arrived yet. Will send you copies when they do. Thaw is here now, but going back to-day or to-morrow.

Love,

KIFFIN.

Escadrille N. 124,

Secteur 24,

Friday, June 23, 1916.

DEAR PAUL:

Well, I feel very blue to-night. Victor was killed this afternoon. I was the guard here to-day and so didn't go out over the lines. The Captain, Victor, Prince and Lufbery went out this afternoon. Inside the German lines they attacked five German machines. The Captain, Prince and Lufbery came out all right and came home. But Victor didn't show up. We were beginning to feel uneasy when a Maurice Farman pilot telephoned that he was there and saw the fight. He said that he saw one of the Nieuports suddenly dive straight down and then the machine break to pieces in air. I figure that Victor was probably hit by a bullet, and that also some of the cables of the machine were cut by bullets. When he was hit he probably fell forward on his "Broom Stick" (or whatever you call in English your *contrôleur);* that would cause the machine to dive, and then if it was weakened by some of the supports being cut would cause what happened. He fell inside the German lines.

If possible, try not to let anything go to the papers in America, until his parents are notified, which we are in train to do. After that, I would like to see every paper in the world pay a tribute to him. There is no question but that Victor had more courage than all the

117

rest of us put together. We were all afraid that he would be killed, and I rooming with him had begged him every night to be more prudent. He would fight every Boche he saw, no matter where or what odds, and I am sure that he had wounded if not killed several. I have seen him twice right on top of a German, shooting hell out of him, but it was always in their lines and there being so much fighting here it is impossible to tell always when you bring down a machine. His head wound was not healed, yet he insisted on flying anyway, and wouldn't take a rest. The first time he was ever in an aëroplane he went as a passenger clear to Dillingham and dropped a bomb on the station there.

Since the war, he never received anything in the way of decorations, yet for this one month here he was proposed for two citations: a l'Ordre de l'Armée, and for the Médaille Militaire.

As I say, he and I roomed together and flew very much together, so I rather feel it, as I had grown to like him very much. I am afraid it is going to rain to-morrow, but if not, Prince and I are going to fly about ten hours, and will do our best to kill one or two Germans for him.

Much love,
KIFFIN.

P.S. The little railroad you asked about still runs, so the lady can go.

Escadrille 124,
Secteur 24,
June 30, 1916.

DEAR MAMMA:

The last week has been too bad weather for any flying. The last day there was anything doing my best friend in the Escadrille was killed—Victor Chapman, the son of John Jay Chapman of New York. He was one of the finest boys I ever knew, the most courageous and the strongest character. His whole family is that way. When his father was told of it, he said: "Very well. He died for a noble cause."

I think the next few days will be great for the Allies, and everyone is very optimistic.

Love to Agnes.

Much love,

KIFFIN.

The following letter was published in "Victor Chapman's Letters from France," with the accompanying note by Mr. John Jay Chapman:

"Of all the men that Victor met in the aviation corps Kiffin Rockwell was the dearest to him. He envied Rockwell for having been in the great charge made by the Legion in May; and worshipped Rockwell's courage and romantic spirit. When Rockwell fell, soon after Victor's death, I felt as if Victor's soul was but a little way above Kiffin's head, and 'stayed for his to keep him company.'

JOHN JAY CHAPMAN."

June 30, 1916.

MY DEAR MRS. CHAPMAN:

I received your letter this morning. I feel mortified that you have had to write me without my having written you before, when Victor was the best friend I ever had. I wanted to write you and his father at once, and tried to a number of times. But I found it impossible to write full justice to Victor or really to express my sympathy with you. Everything I would try to say seemed so weak. So I finally said, "I will just go ahead and work hard, do my best, then if I have accomplished a lot, or been killed in accomplishing it, they will know that I have not forgotten Victor, and that some of his strength of character still lived." There is nothing that I can say to you or anyone that will do full credit to him. And everyone here that knew him feels the same way. To start with, Victor had such a strong character. I think we all have our ideals when we begin, but, unfortunately, there are so very few of us that retain them; and sometimes we lose them at a very early age, and after that, life seems to be spoiled. But Victor was one of the very few who had the strongest of ideals, and then had the character to withstand anything that tried to come into his life and kill them. He was just a large, healthy man, full of life and goodness towards life, and could only

119

see the fine, true points in life and in other people. And he was not of the kind that absorbs from other people, but of the kind that gives out. We all had felt his influence and seeing in him a man made us feel a little more like trying to be men ourselves.

When I am in Paris I stay with Mrs. Weeks, whose son was my friend and killed in the Legion. Well, Victor would come around once in a while to dinner with us. Mrs. Weeks used always to say to me, "Bring Victor around; he does me so much good. I like his laugh and the sound of his voice. When he comes in the room it always seems so much brighter." Well, that is the way it was here in the Escadrille.

For work in the Escadrille, Victor worked hard, always wanting to fly. And courage! He was too courageous; we all would beg him at times to slow up a little. We speak of him every day here, and we have said sincerely amongst ourselves many a time that Victor had more courage than all the rest of the Escadrille combined. He would attack the Germans always, no matter what the conditions or what the odds. The day he was wounded four or five of the Escadrille had been out and come home at the regular hour. Well, Victor had attacked one machine and seriously crippled it, but the machine had succeeded in regaining the German lines. After that, Victor would not come home with the rest but stayed looking for another machine. He found five machines inside our lines. None of us like to see a German machine within our lines without attacking. So, although Victor was alone, he watched the five machines and finally one of them came lower and under him. He immediately dived on this one. Result was that the others dived on him. One of them was a Fokker, painted like the machine of the famous Captain Boelke, and may have been him. This Fokker got the position on Victor and it was a miracle that he was not killed then. He placed bullet after bullet around Victor's head, badly damaging the machine, cutting parts of the command in two, and one bullet cutting his scalp, as you know. Well, Victor got away, and with one hand held the commands together where they had been cut, and landed at Froids, where we had friends in a French Escadrille. There he had dinner and his wound was dressed and they repaired his machine a little. That afternoon he came flying back home with his head all bound up. Yet

120

he thought nothing of it, only smiled and thought it an interesting event. He immediately wanted to continue his work as if nothing had happened. We tried to get him to go to a hospital, or to go to Paris for a short while and rest, but he said No. Then we said, "Well, you have got to take a rest, even if you stay here." The captain told him that he would demand a new and better machine for him and that he could rest while waiting for it to be ready, and then could see whether or not he should go back to flying. This was the *17th* of June. The following morning Balsley was wounded. The same day, or the day after, Uncle Willie came to see Victor and was with us a couple of days. Those first days Victor slept late, a privilege he had not taken before since being in the Escadrille, always having got up at daylight. In the daytime he would be with Uncle Willie or at the field, seeing about his machine, or he would take his old machine and fly over to see Balsley. At first Balsley could not eat or drink anything. But after a few days he was allowed a little champagne and oranges. Well, as soon as Victor found that out, he arranged for champagne to be sent to Balsley and would take oranges over to him. At least once a day, and sometimes twice, he would go over to see Balsley to cheer him up. And in the meantime he wouldn't ever let anyone speak of his wound, as a wound, and was impatient for his new machine. On the 21st he got his machine and had it regulated. On the 22nd he regulated the *mitrailleuse,* and the weather being too bad to fly over the lines, he flew it around here a little to get used to it. His head was still bandaged but he said it was nothing. Late in the afternoon, some German machines were signalled and he went up with the rest of us to look for them, but it was a false alarm. The following morning the weather was good, and he insisted on going out at the regular hour with the rest. There were no machines over the lines, so the "sortie" was uneventful. He came in and at lunch fixed up a basket of oranges which he said he would take to Balsley. We went up to the field and Captain Thénault, Prince and Lufbery got ready to go out and over the lines. Victor put the oranges in his machine and said that he would follow the others over the lines for a little trip and then go and land at the hospital. The Captain, Prince and Lufbery started first. On arriving at the lines they saw at first two German machines which they dived on. When they arrived in the midst of them, they found that two or three other German machines had arrived also. As the odds were against the three they did not fight long, but immediately started back into our lines, and without seeing Victor. When they came back we thought that Victor was at the hospital. But later in the afternoon, a pilot of a Maurice Farman and his passenger sent in a report. The report was that they saw three Nieuports attack five German machines, that at this moment they saw a fourth Nieuport arriving with all speed who dived in the midst of the Germans, that two of the Germans dived toward their field and that the Nieuport fell through the air no longer controlled by the pilot. In a fight it is practically impossible to tell what the other machines do, as everything happens so fast all one can see is the beginning of a fight and then, in a few seconds, the end. That fourth Nieuport was Victor and, owing to the fact that the motor was going full speed when the machine fell, I think he was killed instantly. He died the most glorious death, and at the most glorious time of life to die, especially for him with his ideals. I have never once regretted it for him, as I know he was willing and satisfied to give his life that way if it was necessary, and that he had no fear of death, and there is nothing to fear in death. It is for you, his father, relatives, myself, and for all who have known him, and all who would have known him, and for the world as a whole I regret his loss. Yet he is not dead; he lives forever in every place he has been, and in everyone who knew him, and in the future generations little points of his character will be passed along. He is alive every day in this Escadrille and has a tremendous influence on all our actions. Even the *mécaniciens* do their work better and more conscientiously. And a number of times I have seen Victor's *mécanicien* standing (when there was no work to be done) and gazing off in the direction of where he last saw Victor leaving for the lines.

For promotions and decorations things move slowly in the army, and after it has passed through all the bureaus, it takes some time to get back to you. Victor was proposed for Sergeant and for the Croix de Guerre May 24th. This passed through all the bureaus and was signed by the General, but the papers did not arrive here until June 25th. However, Victor knew on the 23rd that they had passed and that it was only a question of a day or so. He had also been promised, after being wounded, the Médaille Militaire which he would have received some time in July. I wish that they could have sent that to you, for he had gained it, and they would have given it to him. But it is against the rules to give the Médaille Militaire unless everything has been signed before the *titulaire* is killed.

I must close now. You must not feel sorry, but must feel proud and happy.

KIFFIN ROCKWELL.

Written on back of a letter from a friend
July 17, 1916.

DEAR PAUL:

This is all that I found in the letter box. There is no news since you left, except that they pulled off the decoration, but it is nothing elaborate and Wm. [Thaw] has probably told you of it. The weather has been bad, so no flights.

Love,
KIFFIN.

Escadrille N. 124,
Secteur 24,
Sunday, July 23, 1916.

DEAR PAUL:

Have been rather busy lately flying. Friday had a very interesting day. Flew six hours, and attacked four different machines. The first one certainly had a lot of luck. Right over the lines I attacked him first. Went within ten or twenty meters of him, shot forty-four rounds straight into him, then turned off. Lieut. de Laage then arrived just as close to him and shot over eighty shots into him; then came Bert Hall with about twenty more shots, but the d——d Boche went on as if nothing had happened. In the middle of the day Bert and I went out alone. I found an *Aviatik* and dived on him. Two Fokkers dived on me; Bert dived on the two Fokkers, and two more Fokkers went on him. In that line of battle we went down through the air about two thousand meters. I got within about ten meters of my *Aviatik*, shot all my shots into him, and he began to fall in the clouds, and then I disappeared in the clouds.

123

Kiffin RockwellRegulating Machine Gun, before Flight over Verdun Battlefields, July, 1916

I thought that I had gotten the *Aviatik,* but a post of observation that saw the fight said he readdressed. As for Bert, he shot his shots into one Fokker, then the other two got right on his back. They came d——d close to getting him, plugged a lot of bullets around him in the machine, but he wasn't touched.

Yesterday, I flew for over eight hours. One machine attacked by the Lieut. de Laage, Hill and me was forced to land immediately in the German lines. We gave Hill the credit for it, as he was the closest to the German, and more likely to have hit him. But it doesn't count anything officially, but will help him toward a citation.

None of this for publication. I only write it that it might interest you. If the weather keeps up I hope to get an official German most any time.

Love,
KIFFIN.

July 26, 1916.

DEAR MAMMA:

Have been so busy for the last week that I haven't kept up with anything going on around me. The weather has been fine and I have flown between forty and fifty hours over the lines, and have attacked over twenty German machines, shooting a lot of them up very badly, but never having the luck for one of them to fall over the trenches.

What time I have not been in the air I have not had energy enough even to look at a paper, but from what I hear, things are going well for us.

The old Legion has been doing some heavy fighting in the Somme and there is not much left of it, although I hear it did very wonderful work.

Paul and Mrs. Weeks did not go to Normandy, as I thought, but are still in Paris.

Much love,
KIFFIN.

Escadrille N. 124,
Secteur 24,
Thursday, July 27, 1916.

DEAR PAUL:

Am pretty disgusted; have been working my poor head off lately, and don't even get thank-you for it. I may ask any day to change Escadrilles. Everyone here is scrapping and discontented, and I am about the worst of any.

I have had about twenty fights lately, sometimes going as close as ten meters to the Germans, and I almost ran into one two or three days ago. But I haven't had the luck to have one of them smash to pieces in our trenches, so as far as thanks go could not have done anything.

This morning Lieut. de Laage and I brought one down in their lines. I attacked him first and he went over on his nose. As he came up, the Lieut. opened up on him and he fell. The Lieut. deserves all the credit one gives him, but I certainly ran the most risk this morning, and if I didn't hit him myself, which I may have, I made it possible for the Lieut. to hit him. Yet do you think I got any credit for it? Not at all!

Fifteen minutes later I made another German land just within his own lines, having attacked two, and was seen by Prince, but nothing is said about it. The trouble is that I fight all the time, instead of trying to curry favor in useful quarters.

I had a hell of a scrap with the captain about the *popote* right after you left, and refused to have anything more to do with it.

I think the best thing I can do is to go to another Escadrille, but I hate to lose what work I have done here, and to tell you the truth, I want the Légion d'Honneur and a Sous-Lieut.'s grade. I don't give a d—— how conceited it may appear, but I think I have well earned the two.

Love,
KIFFIN.

Escadrille N. 124,
Secteur 24,
Monday, July 31, 1916.

DEAR PAUL:

Received your letter this morning. The weather was good yesterday and to-day, but my machine is worn out, and I won't do much until I get a new one. They are repairing it now, but the Captain made a demand Tor a new one for me, as he couldn't help it, owing to the amount of flying I have done. I took out another machine yesterday, but couldn't do any good with it, as it was not arranged right for me.

Right now I don't care to take a *permission,* as I want to keep up with everything that goes on around here. I want to be changed to a French Escadrille unless certain conditions change here, and several others will follow my example.

I think I have the most hours of flight and the most fights for the month of July on the Verdun front of any Nieuport pilot, but am not sure. I don't think, however, that a full report of my work has gone out of this office, and a number of times my report on a fight has been changed. The machine that Hall brought down X. did his best to prove that it wasn't brought down, and so far Bert hasn't even been proposed for a citation.

Lufbery is a quiet boy who does good work and when he says he has done something we all believe him. This morning Lufbery brought down a German machine ten kilometers in the German lines. We all know he did because he wouldn't lie about it, yet not a soul saw it. Thénault immediately went in an automobile to the Commandant of the Armée, and proposed Lufbery for the Médaille. All of us will be damned glad to see him get it, as he deserves it.

Jim has been fighting a great deal lately; yesterday he got his machine badly hit.

I received a letter of felicitations for my Médaille from Georges de Fontenailles. Tell him I thank him and send my regards.

Much love,
KIFFIN.

August 4, 1916.

DEAR MAMMA:

The weather has remained good for a very long time now, but to-day it looks like bad weather which will probably last several days.

I have been waiting for a new machine and have had a few days of rest.

Last month, in spite of much bad weather, I flew eighty-one hours over the lines and had between thirty and forty fights with German machines, an official report being made on twenty-one of the fights. All, however, were in the German lines, so it was impossible to know the real results.

The Escadrille has done some good work the last few days and brought down several machines.

The news from all the front is good, but still no one has any idea when the war will end, and people seem to worry less about it. To fight has grown to be a kind of habit, and I don't suppose we'd know what else to do.

Much love,

KIFFIN.

Escadrille N. 124,

Secteur 24,

Friday, Aug. 4, 1916.

DEAR PAUL:

In regard to the news from this escadrille and all, I think you had better fix up an arrangement with Jim or someone to keep you posted, or quit trying to handle it. When I have a machine that flies all right, I fly two or three times more than most of them, and for that reason don't have time to write letters or think much about it, and I don't go to Bar-le-Duc once a week whenever I am flying, whereas the others do. Then another thing, you never know when a machine brought down is official or not, and I don't care to write about them when they are not; and then again we are not supposed to publish a history in America of the actions each day of the outfit, although that is practically what happens.

Last month, I had from thirty to forty fights, twenty-one of them being officially reported, yet they did not give me credit for any machines brought down, so I don't see why they should be written up, as after one or two are told of it is the same with all. Now this morning, Lufbery and Jim attacked a machine which they think fell;

later Lufbery and some pilot from a French escadrille had the same experience. Then Bert Hall thinks he brought one down also. Yet so far none of them is officially confirmed, so they may report three machines brought down or they may not report any. Sometimes they report a machine brought down without anyone seeing it, and then again they don't.

One day, Lieut. de Laage and I attacked two machines. At the end of the fight he went straight down and I thought the pilot had been killed, but he readdressed close to the ground with nothing wrong. He was seen going down by a post of observation which did not see him readdress. This post sent in a report that a German machine had been brought down in the German lines. They wanted to give us credit for the machine but we both knew we had not brought down a machine, and told them so, and explained the circumstances. Yet two well-known French pilots claimed it the following day, and were given credit as having brought down a German machine. So all in all, you can't tell much about what is going on in the aviation. Sometimes a man will work his head off and get no credit or recompense, and then later, when he least expects it, he will get everything. I worked d——d hard last month and got no credit for it. Well, now I am going to take it easier this month and I bet I gain more by it. I stayed in bed this morning until ten-thirty, and am taking life easy at present until they give me a new machine.

Love,
KIFFIN.

Escadrille N. 124,
Monday, Aug. 1916.

DEAR PAUL:

Johnson and Hill are going in on *permission.* I will give them this note and they will tell you all the news and just what is going on.

Lufbery brought down a machine this morning that burned up over the trenches. Lufbery is a very good man and we all like to see him get credit for all his work. He has been very lucky in his combats, and this is officially counted as his fourth Boche. Johnson will tell you all about it.

Love,

KIFFIN.

Escadrille N. 124,
Secteur 24,
Wednesday, Aug. 30, 1916.

DEAR PAUL:

I am sending you copies of my, Thaw's and Hall's citations which have just arrived. Also I am sending you a card from Dr. Meade and a letter from Bob Knott. You like to write letters so might answer them, as I have about twenty to write that I put off every day.

It has been bad weather for the last few days so nothing doing. Hope things are going well with you.

Much love,

KIFFIN.

Escadrille N. 124,
Secteur 24,
Friday, Sept. 1, 1916.

DEAR PAUL:

It has been bad weather ever since I have been back, except late yesterday afternoon. I went out then and found a number of Germans and fought with them for a long time, but couldn't do much as I was all alone.

We are getting ready to leave here, and are going by Le Bourget, everyone to get new machines. Will be there two or three days, which time will be spent in Paris. Probably leave here in two or three days. I don't like it much for I lose all the work I have done here, as far as citations or anything go. If anyone asks you where we are going, say Dunkirk, although that is not right.

No one thinks X—— got a German, in fact, everyone is sure he didn't; yet the Captain proposed him for a citation, wanted to propose him for the Médaille, but everyone said if he did they would quit. I am going to have to call him out when he gets back, as he talked awfully big about us behind my back when I was away. We

130

have all agreed to try to run him out of the Escadrille. Will tell you all in Paris.

Love,

KIFFIN.

Sept. 2, 1916.

DEAR MAMMA:

Well, I had a very nice eight days in Paris and feel much better after the rest. Since I got back the weather has made it impossible to do much work. To-morrow will be our last day's work in this sector, as we are moving to some other sector. Will leave here Monday and go by way of Paris, stop there for a few days to get all new machines and then fly to our new location.

Before leaving here they are proposing me Tor another citation in the order of the army, which pleases me. It means another palm on my Croix de Guerre and shows appreciation of the work I have done.

The news is very good now and every one is happy.

Much love,

KIFFIN.

Escadrille N. 124,
Secteur 24,
Monday, Sept. 4, 1916.

DEAR PAUL:

We had expected to leave for Paris to-day, but new orders came in, so now we can only wait. May leave any day. Lieut. de Laage came in to-day, said he was supposed to have dinner with you to-night but didn't have time to let you know, as he returned here immediately on hearing that we were leaving. He is going back in to-night so you will probably see him. No news, except the Captain has proposed me for a citation "à l'Ordre de l'Armée" for my work here. I think it will go through.

Love,

KIFFIN.

Escadrille N. 124,
Secteur 24,
Saturday, Sept. 9, 1916.

DEAR PAUL:

Just a few lines. We have not left yet, but home to be in Paris in a couple of days. This morning I attacked a Boche at three thousand meters high, killed the *observateur* the first shot. After that, followed the machine down to eighteen hundred meters, riddling it with bullets. At that height I was attacked at very close range by two other German machines. I succeeded in getting back home. My first machine fell just in the German trenches, and our artillery fired on it.

Love,
KIFFIN.

Sept. 14, 1916.

DEAR MAMMA:

Well, I am in Paris again. We stayed at Bar-le-Duc a week longer than we expected, but I didn't mind it. Last Saturday morning I brought down a German machine which fell in their first-line trenches. I am proposed for sous-lieutenant for having done it, and am well pleased.

We don't know where we are going and are waiting here for orders. We fear we are going to Luxeuil, where we were last Spring. I like the town, but right now I should prefer going to the Somme.

Mrs. Weeks has just gotten back from England. She had a good time there but says it is a lot of trouble to travel now.

Paul is well.

Much love,
KIFFIN.

Grand Hôtel de la Pomme d'Or,
Luxeuil-les-Bains,
Wednesday, Sept. 20, 1916.

DEAR PAUL:

Received your letter this morning. The weather has been cold and bad ever since we arrived here. I have gotten my machine, which is the best they have, and have fixed it up with two machine-guns. But I don't expect much work here, as I think the weather is going to be bad most of the time. I found a number of people glad to see me back, and think that I can get along all right if we are forced to stay for the winter.

At present am staying at this hotel, but am looking around for a nice quiet little place to live, unless Captain Happe tries to make us live at the field, which will be foolish.

Nothing new of my proposition. Should hear now in a few days. The Captain said that the only thing that could stop it was that a foreigner was supposed to have the grade of sous-off. for one year before passing officer, unless he came to France as an officer, but that is bunk.

Love,
KIFFIN.

CHAPTER IV

KIFFIN ROCKWELL and Lufbery were the first to get their new machines ready and on the 23rd of September went out for the first flight since the escadrille had arrived at Luxeuil. They became separated in the air but each flew on alone, which was a dangerous thing to do in the Alsace sector. There is but little fighting in the trenches there, but great air activity. Due to the British and French squadrons at Luxeuil, and the threat their presence implied, the Germans had to oppose them by a large fleet of fighting machines. I believe there were more than forty Fokkers alone in the camps of Colmar and Habsheim. Observation machines protected by two or three fighting planes would venture far into our lines. It is something the Germans dare not do on any other part of the front. They had a special trick that consisted in sending a large, slow observation machine into our lines to invite attack. When a French plane would dive after it, two Fokkers, that had been hovering high overhead, would drop on the tail of the Frenchman and he stood but small chance if caught in the trap.

Just before Kiffin Rockwell reached the lines he spied a German machine under him, flying at 11,000 feet. I can imagine the satisfaction he felt in at last catching an enemy plane in our lines. Rockwell had fought more combats than the rest of us put together, and had shot down many German machines that had fallen in their lines, but this was the first time he had had an opportunity of bringing down a Boche in our territory.

A captain, the commandant of an Alsatian village, watched the aerial battle through his field glasses. He said that Rockwell approached so close to the enemy that he thought there would be a collision. The German craft, which carried two machine-guns, had opened a rapid fire when Rockwell started his dive. He plunged through the stream of lead and only when very close to his enemy did he begin shooting. For a second it looked as though the German was falling, so the captain said, but then he saw the French machine turn rapidly nose down, the wings of one side broke off and fluttered in the wake of the airplane, which hurtled earthward in a rapid drop. It crashed into the ground in a small field—a field of flowers—a few hundred yards back of the trenches. It was not more than two and a half miles from the spot where Rockwell, in the month of May, brought down his first enemy machine. The Germans immediately opened up on the wreck with artillery fire. In spite of the bursting shrapnel, gunners from a nearby battery rushed out and recovered poor Rockwell's broken body. There was a hideous wound in his breast where an explosive bullet had torn through. A surgeon who examined the body, testified that if it had been an ordinary bullet Rockwell would have had an even chance of landing with only a bad wound. As it was, he was killed the instant the unlawful missile exploded.

Lufbery engaged a German craft but before he could get to close range two Fokkers swooped down from behind and filled his aëroplane full of holes. Exhausting his ammunition he landed at Fontaine, an aviation field near the lines. There he learned of Rockwell's death and was told that two other French machines had been brought down within the hour. He ordered his gasoline tank filled, procured a full band of cartridges and soared up into the air to avenge his comrade. He sped up and down the lines, and made a wide detour to Habsheim where the Germans have an aviation field, but all to no avail. Not a Boche was in the air.

The Spot Where Kiffin Fell, Near Thann, Alsace

The news of Rockwell's death was telephoned to the escadrille. The captain, lieutenant and a couple of men jumped in a staff car and hastened to where he had fallen. On their return the American pilots were convened in a room of the hotel and the news was broken to them. With tears in his eyes, the captain said: "The best and bravest of us all is no more."

No greater blow could have befallen the escadrille. Kiffin was its soul. He was loved and looked up to not only by every man in our flying corps but by everyone who knew him. Kiffin was imbued with the spirit of the cause for which he fought and gave his heart and soul to the performance of his duty. He said: "I pay my part for Lafayette and Rochambeau," and he gave the fullest measure. The old flame of chivalry burned brightly in this boy's fine and sensitive being. With his death France lost one of her most valuable pilots. When he was over the lines the Germans did not pass—and he was over them most of the time. He brought down four enemy planes that were credited to him officially, and Lieutenant de Laage, who was his fighting partner, says he is convinced that Rockwell accounted for many others which fell too far within the German lines to be observed. Rockwell had been given the Médaille Militaire and the Croix de Guerre, on the ribbon of which he wore four palms representing the four magnificent citations he had received in the order of the army. As a further reward or his excellent work he had been proposed for promotion from the grade of sergeant to that of second lieutenant Unfortunately the official order did not arrive until a few days following his death.

The night before Rockwell was killed he had stated that if he were brought down he would like to be buried where he fell. It was impossible, however, to place him in a grave so near the trenches. His body was draped in a French flag and brought back to Luxeuil. He was given a funeral worthy of a general. His brother, Paul, who had fought in the Legion with him, and who had been rendered unfit for service by a wound, was granted permission to attend the obsequies. Pilots from all nearby camps flew over to render homage to Rockwell's remains. Every Frenchman in the aviation at Luxeuil marched behind the bier The British pilots, followed by a detachment of five hundred of their men were in line, and a battalion of French troops brought up the rear. As the slow-moving procession of blue- and khaki-clad men passed from the church to the graveyard aëroplanes circled at a feeble height above and showered down myriads of flowers.

II

Captain Georges Thénault's speech at the graveside was brief and moving; the following translation conveys but a slight idea of the soldierly simplicity and sincerity with which it was delivered:

Here by this tomb so recently closed, we meet to-day to pay our final duty to our comrade

Sergeant Kiffin Rockwell was born in Newport, in the South of the United States. The descendant of an ancient family of soldiers, among whom was one of Washington's officers, who distinguished himself in the War of Independence and later several officers who distinguished themselves during the War of Secession, he received a thorough military training, which gave him the imprint that characterized his life.

Learning of the cowardly aggression of which our country was the object, and loving France as a second motherland, he, with his brother, here present, hastened to France to enlist in the Foreign Legion. He took part in the combats of Artois, in May, 1915, and after a valiant charge of four kilometers, fell, wounded in the thigh, near Neuville-Saint-Vaast, of glorious memory. Immediately on his recovery he joined the aviation corps, where he obtained his brevet in an exceptionally short space of time. On the formation of the American escadrille, he came with it to Luxeuil. Here he at once attracted attention. On May 18th of this year he was the first at Hartmannsweilerkopf to engage in battle, in which he was victorious. Shortly afterwards, for his services, he was awarded the military medal. Ordered to Verdun, he took part in every expedition against the enemy. He was happy in the midst of danger; the greater the strength or the number of the enemy, the more anxious was he to attack. Never did Rockwell consider that he had done enough.

His courage was sublime and when the flights prescribed by the Commandant were accomplished he would set out again on his

The Grave of Kiffin Rockwell at Luxeuil, Alsace

"Baby," barely allowing his mechanic time to refill his tanks.

Indefatigable, he would fly over Vaux and Douaumont, above the crash of the enemy's guns. Where Rockwell was the German could not pass, but was forced rapidly to take shelter on the ground. Daily he compelled enemy airships to descend on their own territory, far behind their lines, his own machine returning with the glorious marks of these encounters.

One day an explosive bullet struck him in the face. He would take no rest, despite the advice of his chiefs, but returned to the combat and brought down one more enemy machine within our lines.

He was a great soldier with a high sense of duty. This he accomplished simply and valiantly, without boasting and without ambition. "I am paying my part of our debt to Lafayette and Rochambeau," he would say. He gave himself to France and for France he sacrificed himself.

On September 23, immediately on his return to Luxeuil, he burned with a desire to fly over the fields of Alsace. He flew over them and not far from the spot where he fought his first glorious battle, he attacked the enemy. But there, cruel fate willed it that he, Rockwell, who for four months fought at Verdun; who single-handed attacked ten enemy machines, should fall with a bullet in his chest as he advanced to meet his adversary.

Glory be to him who fell valiantly in the pursuit of his dream of love and justice. He met the glorious death he so much desired. On the night of his death, when we were gathered together, I said to his comrades, "The best and bravest of us all is no longer here." And never was commendation more merited.

Glory be to his noble family and to his brother, whom a serious wound has forced to leave the field of battle. We share in their great sorrow.

And to thee, our best friend, in the name of France I bid thee a last farewell. In the name of thy comrades, who have so often proved that they know how to keep their promises, I salute thee reverently. And with the memory of those who have already fallen, and whom we here invoke, we swear faithfully to guard thy memory and to avenge it.

III

Kiffin Rockwell's death was recounted and commented upon by the press of every civilized country in the world. Of the thousands of articles written, none were finer or expressed with more feeling than two news stories by Paul Scott Mowrer cabled to the Chicago *Daily News,* and an unsigned editorial from the Charleston (South Carolina) *News and Courier,* which are reproduced below:

PARIS, FRANCE, September 25.—When Kiffin Yates Rockwell, American airman in the service of France, and brother of Paul Ayres Rockwell, of the *Daily News* staff of war correspondents, fell in an aëroplane duel in the Vosges, his life ended as he himself would have preferred.

The death of a friend is always a shock, but Rockwell's death was not a surprise. In tireless and excessive intrepidity he almost seemed to have courted it only as a means of fighting for the cause of France, which was dearer to him than life.

Since leaving the Foreign Legion for the air service, Rockwell had brought down four German aëroplanes officially and probably others which dropped uncounted inside the enemy lines. He had been decorated with the war cross and the military medal; he was frequently mentioned in the order of the day and he was recently proposed for promotion as lieutenant. While stationed in the Verdun region he was more hours in the air than any other aviator in the French Army. In a struggle of this kind such devotion and zeal have their price; it is invariably the bravest who fall.

Kiffin Yates Rockwell came of an old American Southern family with a French strain in its blood. His ancestors distinguished themselves in two wars. His own appearance did not belie his descent. Tall, straight and slender, with something of the look of the falcon in his sensitive face, he seemed at times the embodiment of the spirit of battle. His nerves were high strung, but always under the control of his unswerving will. He hid the fire of his emotions behind a smiling taciturnity.

Unlike most soldiers, he objected even to being talked about, and the publicity which the correspondents have given the American air squadron was abhorrent to him.

"Why should we be written up," he would ask, almost fiercely, "for doing what our French comrades do as well every day?"

A few days ago he was in Paris and I had luncheon with him and his brother. At first he spoke little, but as the conversation turned on air-flights his eyes suddenly blazed, and smiling his peculiar smile, he said:

"We fly alone, while their pilots are accompanied by special machine-gun operators, yet it is a fair fight. Our superior skill and initiative make us a match for them."

Later, he said, still in the same soft Georgian drawl:

"An aviator need not know much about the works of his machine. He only needs to know how to fly. The rest he can leave to his mechanic. Aviators who know too much about their craft are usually nervous. They understand what it means when the motor makes a funny noise. We others go on flying, blissfully ignorant and hoping for the best."

Finally, we spoke of death, and I remarked:

"The man who enters this war should consider himself dead from that moment. Every day thereafter that he lives should be accounted as so much good luck—as so much to be grateful for."

Rockwell made no answer but looked me straight in the eye with his mysterious smile. This man did not fear death, for he had faced it too often. He was brave among the brave, and besides, he loved the cause—the cause of France, which for him was the cause of all mankind.

By Paul Scott Mowrer.

(Special Cable to the Chicago *Daily News)*

Paris, September 29.—This is the story of how Kiffin Yates Rockwell died, as it was told to me by his brother, Paul, who has just returned from burying the heroic aviator.

The American air squadron was transferred recently from Verdun to a sector in Alsace, where the enemy, fearing raids into Germany, keep many of their fighting planes. Kiffin Rockwell was one of the first men ready for work in the new sector. He mounted two machine-guns on his aëroplane and last Saturday morning started out alone to look for German machines. He found one almost immediately. A new model *Aviatik* carrying a pilot and two gunners had flown inside the French lines.

Rockwell, from a superior height, swooped down upon the German machine. An infantry officer watching through glasses from the trenches heard the exchange of shots and saw the two machines rush swiftly together. For a moment he thought the German craft had been wrecked; then he saw the French machine tilt and plunge. One wing was torn off in the speed of the descent and drifted sideways for nearly a kilometer (more than half a mile) on the breeze, while the aëroplane itself, from a height of three and a half kilometers (two miles) dropped like a stone and struck near a little wood just behind the lines.

The Germans had seen the occurrence and began to bombard the spot. Nevertheless, some soldiers ran out and, braving the shells, found that the machine in falling had dug a hole in the ground a yard deep and several yards wide.

Two soldiers carried the body of the aviator into the trenches, where a doctor certified that Rockwell had been shot through the chest with an explosive bullet and had died instantly. An ordinary bullet would probably only have wounded him. This bullet, bursting as it did, tore a fearful gash.

News of Rockwell's death spread quickly. Lufbery, another American, who had started out at the same time that Rockwell did, but in a different direction, had exhausted his ammunition in a desperate fight with three German machines and had been forced to land. The wings of his machine were full of holes, but on learning his comrade's fate he borrowed a fresh belt of cartridges and rose again immediately in a vain effort to overtake the fatal *Aviatik*.

When Rockwell's body was brought into the camp the squadron captain called the men together and after praising the dead American in the highest terms said that, however great their grief at losing a man who had been a noble example and a true friend to every one, their entire effort must now be devoted to avenging him. All then swore an oath of vengeance.

A French lieutenant, who frequently flew with Rockwell and was his most constant friend and admirer, wept like a child. Indeed, every man wept, for Rockwell had been the life and soul of the squadron. In a single month at Verdun he had fought thirty-four victorious fights, often against odds. He had brought down two Germans inside the French lines, two near the trenches and about six inside the German lines.

Some days before his death he had specified that if he should be killed by the Germans, whatever money was found on him should be used by the squadron to drink to the destruction of the Germans. This was solemnly done. A bottle of old Bourbon whisky which had been given Rockwell by an American in Paris, will be opened hereafter when members of the squadron bring down Germans. On these occasions a few drops will be poured out for the victor in honor of Rockwell's memory and then the bottle will be resealed.

Three Americans flew out on Sunday morning, bent on vengeance, but were unable to find a German machine.

In a cemetery near the front, Kiffin Yates Rockwell was buried with full military honors. Several well-known aviators followed the flower-decked gun carriage, which bore the coffin wrapped in a flag, on which were pinned the victim's medals. One famous flyer said that Rockwell's death was the severest loss French aviation had suffered in many a day.

Paul Rockwell has brought back to Paris a small box in which are a few pathetic articles his brother had on him at the time of his death. Among them are the war cross and the military medal, a fountain pen, some personal letters, an unbroken wrist-watch, which had stopped at 9:50 o'clock, and a silver cigarette case, crushed and bent fantastically.

There are also a few pressed crocuses, for it was in a bank of these flowers beside a tinkling stream in a gentle Alsatian valley, not far from Thann, that the aviator's body was found.

"He always said that in case of death he wished to be buried where he fell," Paul Rockwell told me. "There is no lovelier spot in the world. I have marked it carefully and after the war I shall remove him from the cemetery to that flowery bank. I hope then to be able to pass a part of every year near him there."

By Paul Scott Mowrer.
(Special Cable to the Chicago Daily News)

ACCOUNT OF DEATH

AN UNSIGNED EDITORIAL FROM THE CHARLESTON
"NEWS AND COURIER"

Kiffin Rockwell of Atlanta, who met his death Saturday morning in an aerial duel with a German airman must have had in his veins the blood of some knight-errant of the age of chivalry. Why should this young Southerner have given his gallant life to France? Perhaps because this splendid France of to-day stirred his imagination so powerfully that he could do nothing less than offer her his sword as Lafayette offered us his in our fight for liberty. Perhaps because he was one of those restless spirits to which life without adventure is but a sad and monotonous pilgrimage.

At any rate, he has met the end that comes to most knights-errant whether they are spurred on by loyalty to some fine ideal or whether their incentive is simply that lust for adventure that all men possess in greater or less degree. Yet before the end came to him, how wonderful was the life that he contrived to live in this age of the world that only a little while ago seemed to be of all ages the least fruitful of perilous adventure. He had fought with the Foreign Legion until that famous organization was practically wiped out. Transferred then, at his own request, to the flying corps, he had engaged in thirty-four battles in the air in less than as many days. The military medal was his—in honor of a notable air victory last May. He had enjoyed the amazing experience of combat in the clouds with a hostile air cruiser while beneath him on the earth raged the momentous battle of Verdun, the greatest battle that the world had ever seen. He had been a participant in what was perhaps the most marvelous episode of a war which has been an uninterrupted succession of marvels—a general fleet action in the air between almost the whole Franco-American squadron of aerial cruisers and a strong force of German aircraft. When the end came for him in combat with a German airman over Alsace, he was playing a part in another episode scarcely less wonderful—an expedition of air cruisers against one of the strongholds of the enemy.

We are all creatures of circumstance and of environment. Many and various, and in most cases humdrum and commonplace enough, are the activities of the modern prototypes of those young Southerners who rode with Stuart and Hampton. But that is not true

145

of all of them. One of them has just ridden to a soldier's death on a steed swifter than the finest charger that ever bore Jeb Stuart to battle.

IV

The following article is representative of the comment by the French Press, *L'Illustration*, Oct. 6, 1916, on Kiffin Rockwell:

L'AVIATEUR KIFFIN ROCKWELL MORT POUR LA FRANCE

L'Aviateur américain, Kiffin Rockwell, a été tué dans un combat aérien près de Thann. Il avait vingt-quatre ans. Il appartenait à une des familles les plus connues et les plus estimées de la Caroline du Nord. Il avait fait des brillantes études à l'Institut Militaire de Washington et Lee Université de Virginie.

Le jour de la déclaration de guerre, son frère Paul et lui écrivaient à notre consul à la Nouvelle Orléans pour offrir leurs services a la France. Le 7 Août, ils s'embarquaient à New York, et le 27 Août il s'engageaient dans la Légion Etrangère. Ils firent la guerre ensemble sur l'Aisne et en Champagne, puis sils se separèrent. Kiffin Rockwell alla dans l'Artois. En Avril, 1915, il écrivait à son frère, resté dans le secteur de . . .: "Si la France devait être vaincue j'aimerais mieux mourir."

Le 9 Mai de la même année il était grièvement blessé dans l'assaut qui nous rendait maîtres de la Targette.

À peine guéri il entrait dans l'aviation, où il retrouvait ses amis Thaw et Chapman. Ses rares qualités de sangfroid, d'habilité et de courage en faisaient rapidement un pilote accompli. Cinq jours après son arrivée au front, il abattait son premier avion allemand, près de l'Hartmannsweilerkopf. Il partait pour Verdun.... En un seul mois, il livrait trente-quatre combats. Un jour il attaquait seul trois avions ennemis; il était blessé à la tête, mais il sortait vainqueur de la rencontre, ayant obligé un de ses adversaires à atterrir. Le 8 Septembre, il abattait un autre avion allemand qui tombait à Vauquois.

Le 23 Septembre, il trouvait une mort glorieuse sur les lignes d'Alsace.

Le jour de ses obsèques, le capitaine de son escadrille me disait:

"Je n'ai jamais connu de meilleur pilote, de soldat plus brave, ni de nature plus généreuse et plus simple." Son camarade de combat, le Lieutenant de Laage, ajoutait: "Kiffin ignorait le danger et la peur. Il allait au combat comme à une fête. Tous nous l'aimions et l'admirions."

Kiffin Rockwell avait reçu la Médaille Militaire et la Croix de Guerre. Il avait trois citations magnifiques. Il avail été nommé sous-lieutenant, mais sa nomination n'est parvenue à son unité qu'après sa mort.

Le nom de ce jeune héros vivra dans le souvenir ému et reconnaissant de la France.

V

The news of Kiffin Rockwell's death aroused great interest in Germany, as is evidenced by the following dispatch from Berlin to the *Journal de Genève:*

L'AVIATIC ESCADRILLE AMÉRICAINE—ET L'OPINION EN ALLEMAGNE

La nouvelle que le fameux aviateur américain Rockwell a été tué sur le front occidental, où il se trouvait au service des Alliés, a causé en Allemagne une très vive impression.

"Cette nouvelle," écrit la *Deutsche Tageszeitung,* "mérite la plus grande attention. Il ne s'agit pas d'un cas isolé, c'est toute une division d'aviateurs américains qui se sont mis au service de nos ennemis. L'Amérique ne se contente pas de nous combattre en cachette dans la question des sous-marins. Elle participe, désormais, d'une manière active, à la lutte contre nous. Les États-Unis favorisent donc notre ennemi d'une manière contraire à la neutralité. L'Amérique doit savoir notre profonde indignation; elle doit aussi savoir que nous considérons cette participation de ses citoyens a la guerre contre nous comme une provocation directe."

Sur le même objet le *Lokal Anzeiger,* en annonçant que sur le front de Verdun il y a un aviatic squadron américain, rappelle les concessions faites par l'Allemagne à l'Amérique par gain de paix et pour éviter des victimes humaines.

"Or, l'Amérique non seulement profile de ces concessions pour continuer à fournir des munitions et des armes à l'Entente, mais elle en abuse. Des Américains peuvent rejoindre les armées ennemies et y occuper des positions importantes."

Le journal parle de l'esprit d'aventure des Américains; mais on pouvait croire "entre personnes comme il faut" que les concessions accordées auraient mis un frein à l'esprit d'aventure et empêché de franchir les limites de la plus élémentaire neutralité.

VI

After the Armistice, when it was possible to approach the spot where Kiffin Rockwell crashed to earth with his aëroplane, the Alsatian officers who had volunteered in the French Army erected there a commemorative cross. This letter, from Lieutenant Auguste Zundel, of Thann, describes the simple ceremony:

Service des Renseignements,
Belfort, le 25 Decembre, 1918.

CHER MONSIEUR ROCKWELL:

J'ai profité hier matin d'un passage à Rodern pour aller planter la croix avec la plaque à l'endroit où est tombé votre frère. Tous mes camarades Alsaciens m'ont accompagné pour rendre les honneurs à cet ami américain tombé, en Alsace, pour que l'Alsace redevienne française. Nous avons été heureux de pouvoir, en quelque sorte, lui en exprimer ainsi notre reconnaissance.

Le but de notre voyage était de passer la veille de Noël à Mulhouse, pour la première fois depuis cinq ans. Nous ne pouvions mieux faire que de nous rendre auparavant à Rodern pour en rendre hommage à votre frère.

Mes camarades se joignent à moi pour vous faire parvenir nos très cordiales salutations et l'expression de nos sentiments les meilleurs.

A. ZUNDEL.

Ci-joint un croquis de l'emplacement.

ACCOUNT OF DEATH

[Translation]

Service des Renseignements,
Belfort, le 25 Decembre, 1918.

DEAR MR. ROCKWELL:

Yesterday morning I took advantage of my passage through Rodern to go and plant the cross, with a plate, on the spot where your brother fell. All my Alsatian comrades accompanied me to render homage to our American friend who had fallen, in Alsace, that Alsace might once more become French. We were pleased to be able, in some way, to prove to him our gratitude.

The object of our journey was to spend Christmas Eve at Mulhouse, for the first time in five years. We could not do better than go first to Rodern to pay our respects to your brother.

My comrades unite with me in sending our most cordial salutations and the expression of our best sentiments.

A. ZUNDEL.

Herewith sketch of the piece of ground.

CITATIONS

GRAND QUARTIER GÉNÉRAL DES ARMÉES

Au G. Q. G., le 21 Juin, 1916.

État-Major.

ORDRE No. 3108 "D"

La *Médaille Militaire* a été conferée au Militaire dont le nom suit:

Rockwell, Kiffin Yates, Mle 34805
Caporal à l'Escadrille N. 124

Engagé pour la durée de la guerre, a été blessé une premiere fois le 9 Mai, 1915, au cours d'une charge à la baïonnette. Passé dans l'Aviation, s'est montré pilote adroit et courageux. Le 18 Mai, 1916, a attaqué et descendu un avion allemand. Le 24 Mai n'a pas hesité à livrer à plusieurs appareils ennemis un combat au cours duquel il a été atteint d'une grave blessure à la face.

La présente nomination comporte l'attribution de la *Croix de Guerre* avec palme.

(Signé) JOFFRE.

IIᵉ Armée.

Aéronautique.

Extrait de l'Ordre Général No. 429. Le Général Commandant la IIᵉ Armée, cite à l'Ordre de l'Armée:

Rockwell, Kiffin Yates, Pilote à l'Escadrille 124.

CITATIONS

Engage pour la durée de la guerre. Entré dans l'aviation de chasse, s'y est classé immédiatement comme pilote de tout premier ordre, d'une audace et d'une bravoure admirable. N'hesite jamais à attaquer l'ennemi quelque soit le nombre des adversaires qu'il rencontre, l'obligeant le plus souvent par sa maîtrise, son mordant, à abandonner la lutte. A abbatu deux avions ennemis. A rendu les plus grands services à l'aviation de chasse de l'armée en se dépensant pendant quatre mois sans compter devant Verdun.

(Signé) R. NIVELLE.

Le Général Commandant en Chef cite à l'Ordre de l'Armée ROCKWELL, Kiffin Yates, Mle 8048, Sergent à l'Escadrille N. 124:

Pilote américain qui n'a cessé de faire l'admiration de ses camarades par son sang-froid, son courage et son audace. A été tué au cours d'un combat aérien le 23 Septembre, 1916.

Au G. Q. G. le 4 Octobre, 1916.

Le Général Commandant en Chef:

(Signé) J. JOFFRE.

RÉPUBLIQUE FRANÇAISE

Ministère de la Guerre

Ordre National de la Légion d'Honneur

Par arrêt ministériel rendu un application des décrets des 13 Août, 1914, et 1er Octobre, 1918. La Croix de Chevalier dans l'Ordre National de la Légion d'Honneur a été attribuée à la mémoire

du Sous-Lieutenant Rockwell, Kiffin Yates,
du 2e Groupe d'Aviation
MORT POUR LA FRANCE

Pilote américain qui n'a cessé de faire l'admiration de ses chefs et de ses camarades par son sang-froid, son courage et son audace. A été mortellement blessé au cours d'un combat aérien le 23

151

Septembre, 1916. Déjà Médaillé pour faits de guerre.
　(A été cité)

(Signé) Louis Barthou.

Although Kiffin Rockwell had already been decorated with the *Médaille Militaire,* four months before his death, this honor was again bestowed upon him posthumously by the Foreign Legion, with this citation:

Arrête: Est inscrit au tableau spécial de la médaille militaire, à titre posthume, le militaire dont le nom suit:

1ᵉʳ Rég. Étr.

ROCKWELL (Kiffin Yates), mle 34805, sergent-pilote: sous-officier pilote. Aviateur remarquablement brave. Tombé glorieusement pour la France, le 23 Septembre, 1916, en Alsace, au cours d'un combat aérien. *Croix de Guerre* avec étoile d'argent.

(Signé) Rollet.

Le Colonel Commandant le *1ᵉʳ* Régiment Étranger.

Translations

The *Médaille Militaire* is conferred upon Corporal-Pilot Kiffin Yates Rockwell, volunteer for the duration of the war. Wounded first during a bayonet charge, May 9, 1915. Transferred to the aviation service, he has there shown himself a skilful and courageous pilot. May 18, 1916, he attacked and brought down a German aëroplane. May 24th, he did not hesitate to deliver attacks on several enemy machines, during the course of which combat he was painfully wounded in the face.

The present nomination carries with it the *Croix de Guerre* with Palm.

(Signed) Joffre.

Kiffin Yates Rockwell, Sergent-pilot with Escadrille N. 124; enlisted for the duration of the war. Having entered the *aviation de chasse,* he revealed himself immediately to be a pilot of the very first order, of admirable daring and bravery. He never hesitates to attack the enemy, no matter what may be the number of adversaries he encounters, usually obliging the enemy, by the skill and sharpness of his attack, to abandon the struggle. Has destroyed two enemy machines. Has rendered the most valuable services to the *aviation de chasse* of the army by unsparing efforts during four months at Verdun.

(Signed) R. NIVELLE.

Kiffin Yates Rockwell, an American pilot who ceaselessly won the admiration of his chiefs and his comrades by his sang-froid, his courage and his daring. Grievously wounded in the course of an aërial attack, September 23, 1916.

(Signed) JOFFRE.
General-Commander-in-Chief.

The Cross of Chevalier of the National Order of the Legion of Honor has been attributed to the memory of Sous-lieutenant-pilot Kiffin Yates Rockwell, of the Second Aviation Group: He Died for France.

An American pilot who ceaselessly won the admiration of his chiefs and his comrades by his sangfroid, his courage and his daring. Mortally wounded during an aërial combat, September 23, 1916. Already decorated with the *Médaille Militaire* for feats of war. Has been cited.

(Signed) LOUIS BARTHOU.

Is inscribed posthumously on the special table of the *Médaille Militaire:*

Kiffin Rockwell, of the First Foreign Regiment, matriculation number 34805. A remarkably brave pilot aviator. Fell gloriously for France, September 23rd, 1916, in Alsace, in the course of an aerial combat. *Croix de Guerre,* with silver star.

(Signed) ROLLET
Colonel Commanding the First Foreign Regiment.

IN MEMORY OF KIFFIN ROCKWELL

By Edgar Lee Masters

"I pay my debt for Lafayette and Rochambeau."
(Kiffin Rockwell's own words).

Eagle whose fearless
Flight in vast spaces
Clove the inane,
While we stood tearless
White with rapt faces
In wonder and pain.

Heights could not awe you,
Depths could not stay you,
Anguished we saw you,
Saw death waylay you
Where the storm flings
Black clouds to thicken
Round France's defender!
Archangel stricken
From ramparts of splendor—
Shattered your wings!

But Lafayette called you,
Rochambeau beckoned.
Duty enthralled you.
For France you had reckoned
Her gift and your debt.

Dull hearts could harden,
Half-gods could palter,
For you never pardon
If Liberty's altar
You chanced to forget.

Stricken archangel!
Ramparts of splendor
Keep you, evangel
Of souls who surrender
No banner unfurled
For ties ever living,
Where freedom has bound them,
Praise and thanksgiving
For love which has crowned them—
Love frees the world!

APPENDIX

The French *Legion Étrangère,* as it exists to-day, was organized in 1831, although throughout the course of her history France has had foreign troops in her service. The Foreign Legion of 1831 was formed in order to provide employment for the hundreds of political refugees who had flocked to Paris from Poland and other countries, and a royal ordinance decreed that it should be used only in the colonies. The conquest of Algeria was then in progress, so the Legion was immediately sent to northern Africa, which has been its headquarters ever since. The corps has served with distinction in all the French Colonial Wars since 1831, and in Europe during the Spanish and Crimean campaigns, the war of Napoleon III in Italy, and the Franco-Prussian War of 1870. It also played a heroic role during the ill-fated struggle of Maxmilian in Mexico.

When the World War broke out, there were two regiments of the Foreign Legion, including some sixteen thousand men, serving in the French Colonies. These men had all enlisted for five years' service. As thousands of foreigners offered their services to France against Germany in August, 1914, a new law was passed authorizing these volunteers to enlist in the Foreign Legion for the duration of the war. Four new *régiments de marche* were formed in France: the Second, Third and Fourth Marching Regiments of the First Foreign Regiment (the Fourth *Régiment de Marche* was composed entirely of Italian volunteers, known as the Garibaldians), and the Second *Régiment de Marche* of the Second Foreign Regiment.

Veteran Legionnaires were brought to France from the Colonies, to drill the new men, and to form a nucleus of experienced soldiers, necessary to make a valuable fighting machine. For the first year or more, there was considerable jealousy between the old Legionnaires of Colonial service and the volunteers fresh from civilian life. The latter rather looked down upon the veterans as mercenary soldiers, while the old Legionnaires quite justly considered the newcomers as inexperienced and raw. Months of common hardships and danger did away with these petty sentiments, and by the end of 1916, the *Régiment de Marche de la Légion Étrangère* was probably the finest unit in the entire French Army. The four full marching regiments of 1914 had been reduced by terrific losses to one three-battalioned regiment, but this regiment won citation after citation in Army Orders, and covered itself with glory upon every battlefield where it appeared. It finally won the double *fourragère,* in the combined colors of the *Légion d'Honneur* and *Croix de Guerre,* the highest distinction a French regiment can earn.

Kiffin Rockwell first served in the Second Marching Regiment of the Second Foreign Regiment. In this unit were several hundred Russian Jews and Armenians, already afflicted with Bolshevist ideas and their presence and propaganda did much to sap the morale of the other volunteers, and to lessen their confidence in the fighting ability of their regiment. Shortly after Kiffin Rockwell transferred to the Second Marching Regiment of the First Foreign Regiment , the aforementioned Russian Jews mutinied; several were shot and others were sent away from the Legion (some returned to Russia after the revolution, and held important posts under the Bolshevist régime) greatly bettering the morale of the regiment.

The Ninth Squad—*Neuvième Escouade*—frequently mentioned in Kiffin Rockwell's letters, was composed of the tallest men in C Battalion of the Second Marching Regiment: Kiffin and Paul Rockwell, Alan Seeger, Ferdinand Capdevielle, Dennis Dowd, William Thaw, Stewart Carstairs and Frederick Zinn, Americans; two English volunteers, Booth and Buchanan; von Krogh, a Norwegian, and Elov Nilson, a Swede; Hubmajer, a Serbian; Pierre, an old French Legionnaire, and, as chief, a German from Saxony, Corporal Weideman. Most of the *corvées,* or unpleasant tasks, fell upon the shoulders of the Ninth Squad, partly because being tall, its members were the men most easily seen, and partly because Weideman was not popular with his sergeant, who delighted in passing on to him all the work possible.

The Ninth Squad made the longest, hardest forced march that fell to the lot of any unit of Legionnaires in France during the World War. The Second Foreign Regiment had been in the sector around the south side of Reims Mountain, and towards the end of October, 1914, was ordered to another part of the front.

The Ninth Squad was named *"garde de convoi,"* to escort the supply wagons to the new sector; the rest of the regiment went ahead in autobuses. Corporal Weideman lined up his men at the edge of the little hill village of Verzenay (Marne) at 4:30 in the morning. Something was wrong with the kitchen supplies, and no rations were issued, except a half-cup of lukewarm, strong, black coffee per man. Then, behind the mule-drawn supply wagons and carts, the Squad set out, along the vineyard-lined highways, making almost a semicircle around the doomed city of Reims.

Fortunately, the day was sunny, and there was plenty of color and interest along the route. The Division Marocaine was at this part of the front, and the brilliant uniforms of the Zouaves and the native Colonial sharp-shooters had not yet been changed for sober khaki. The Germans were bombarding Reims, and shells could be seen breaking around the cathedral. There was much movement along the highways, and an occasional aëroplane flew overhead.

All this excitement kept fatigue away for hours, but when two o'clock in the afternoon arrived and no halt had been made for lunch—the Squad and supply train paused every fifty minutes for the regulation ten minutes rest—the men began to complain. Grumbling was useless, however; the corporal had his orders, which were to follow the convoy. No bread had been issued; a few of the men had some left of the previous day's ration, and shared this with their comrades.

One of the mule-drivers started the rumor that Fismes was the destination of the Regiment, and that the convoy and its guard would also rest there for the night. By dusk, all the men of the Ninth Squad were footsore and weary, and even the Corporal was walking with a limp. He lost his detached attitude, and admitted that he did not know where a final halt would be made, but stated that he hoped to get orders at Fismes.

APPENDIX

Fismes was reached shortly after dark. No one there had seen or heard anything of the Second Foreign Regiment, but finally, a dispatch-bearing cyclist appeared, and the convoy and guard set forth up the hill towards the Aisne sector. By now the mules themselves could scarcely walk, and their drivers were swearing as vociferously as their exhausted condition would permit. The men of the Ninth Squad were so sodden in misery that they could not complain, but staggered on in a sort of daze. Every half hour, ten-minute halts were made, and the men threw themselves down and slept, on rock piles or anything else at hand to keep them out of the mud.

Finally, at eleven o'clock at night, a real halt was called, on a hillside above Berry-au-Bac, so near the trenches that orders given their men by the French officers could be heard distinctly. A steady machine-gun and rifle fire was going on. Kiffin Rockwell, Alan Seeger and Dennis Dowd were called off by the Corporal, and posted on guard; the rest of the men threw themselves down and tried to sleep.

The Ninth Squad had marched fifty-six kilometers, carrying rifles, cartridges, and other equipment.

A little after four o'clock the next morning, the convoy and guard again set forward, and a few hours later staggered into the tiny hamlet of Cuiry-les-Chaudardes (Aisne), which was to be headquarters for the American Volunteers for some months to come.

NAMES APPEARING IN LETTERS

Balsley, Clyde, of San Antonio, Texas. Balsley was in hospital for almost a year and a half, before he finally recovered from his wound, which left him permanently crippled. He was decorated with the *Médaille Militaire* and the *Croix de Guerre,* with a glowing citation in Army Orders. He returned to America in the autumn of 1917, and despite his disability, offered "his services to the United States; he was commissioned captain and was very useful, attached to the Pursuit Division, United States Air Service.

Buchanan; an English volunteer in the Foreign Legion. He transferred to the British Army in 1915.

Capdevielle, Ferdinand, of New York City, known as "Cap" to his comrades of the Legion. He transferred to the 170th French Line

Regiment in October, 1915, and at Verdun in 1916 was first promoted corporal, then sergeant, and was decorated with the *Croix de Guerre* for gallant conduct during the retaking of the Bois de Caillette, near Verdun. When Kiffin Rockwell was killed, Capdevielle wrote as follows to Paul Rockwell:

"While at the front I read in the papers that Kiffin had died serving under the French flag. It is, I must say, a very-hard blow to you, Paul, but what do you want, we have at times to part with what we love best.

For my part, I must say that I respected Kiffin more than any other American I have ever known, and although I am very grieved at his death, I am proud to say that I was a friend of an American hero who did not think twice of offering his life."

Capdevielle did not transfer to the United States Army after his country entered the ranks against Germany, although offered a good commission as officer. He declared that he had started out in the war under the French flag, and that he would end his military career there. He won the rank of sous-lieutenant in the 170th Line Regiment, and was killed on October 3, 1918, leading his men in a charge against the German machine-gun nests at Orfeuil (Champagne).

Capdevielle was the last of the American Volunteers of 1914 to fall in battle, and was posthumously awarded the Cross of the Legion of Honor, with the following brilliant citation:

"Capdevielle, Ferdinand, Sous-Lieutenant, brillant officier. Citoyen américain, engagé volontaire au service de la France dès le début de la guerre. A participé tant à la Légion Etrangère qu'au *170ème* R. I., à toutes les batailles importantes de la campagne. A toujours fait l'admiration de ses hommes et conquis l'estime de ses chefs par ses vertus militaires et morales. Le 3 Octobre, 1918, chargé d'enlever à l'assaut le peloton de tête de sa compagnie, est parti superbement, progressant malgré un feu extrêmement violent de mitrailleuses ennemis, qu'il tenta de reduire immédiatement par la manœuvre et le feu de ses pièces. Est tombé glorieusement, frappé d'une balle à la tête, à l'instant même où il se dressait debout pour enlever ses hommes à l'assaut de la position ennemie. A été cité."

Translation: Capdevielle, Ferdinand, Sous-Lieutenant, brilliant officer. American citizen, volunteered his services for France at the outbreak of the war. Took part, both in the Foreign Legion and in the 170th Infantry Regiment, in all the important battles of the campaign. Won the admiration of his men and the esteem of his chiefs by his military and moral qualities. On October 3rd, 1918, ordered to rescue the platoon at the head of his company from the assault of the enemy, he departed in superb style, advancing despite the extremely violent fire of the enemy mitrailleuses, which he sought to reduce by maneuvering his own machine-guns. Fell gloriously, struck by a bullet in the head at the very instant he was about to rescue his men from the enemy's position."

Casey, John Jacob, of San Francisco. An artist who had lived in Paris for a number of years before the war. He was wounded during the Champagne offensive, September 25, 1915, but after a short stay in hospital, recovered and returned to the front, where he remained until the end of 1917, when he was liberated from the Legion in order to join the United States Army. Casey was cited in Army Orders, and decorated with the *Croix de Guerre*.

Chapman, Victor Emmanuel, of New York City. Chapman was cited in Army Orders as follows:

"Citoyen américain, engage pour la durée de la guerre. Pilote remarquable par son audace, s'elançant sur les avions ennemis quelqu'il en soit le nombre, et quelque soit l'altitude. Le 24 Mai, a attaqué seul trois avions allemands; a livré un combat au cours duquel il a eu ses vêtements traversés de plusieurs balles et a été blessé au bras."

"Pilote de Chasse qui était un modèle d'audace, d'energie et entrain, et faisait l'admiration de ses camarades d'escadrille. Sérieusement blessé à la tete le 17 Juin, a demandé de ne pas interrompre son service. Quelques jours plus tard s'étant lancé à l'attaque de plusieurs avions ennemis, a trouvé une mort glorieuse au cours de la lutte."

Victor Chapman was posthumously awarded the *Médaille Militaire*. His letters to his family were published in book form.

Chatkoff, Herman Lincoln, of Brooklyn, N. Y. Chatkoff transferred from the Legion to the Aviation in May, 1916. Shortly after he began flying at the front, in June, 1917, he was badly injured in an aëroplane accident near Chaudon, and was incapacitated for further service. He was decorated with the *Croix de Guerre.*

Dowd, Dennis, of Brooklyn, N. Y., a young lawyer, graduate of Georgetown and Columbia Universities, who sailed for France at the outbreak of the war in August, 1914, and enlisted in the Legion. He was wounded during the Champagne battle, October, 1915, and upon recovery transferred to the Aviation. He was killed in a flying accident at Buc, near Paris, on August 12, 1916, the first American volunteer to die at a French aviation training school.

Drossner, Carl Jean. A California Jew, who deserted from the Foreign Legion after a few weeks at the Lyons training camp. He was in prison in Chicago, towards the end of 1918, on the charge of passing a worthless cheque.

Eyre, Lincoln, Paris Correspondent of the New York *World,* during the war.

Farnsworth, Henry Weston, of Dedham, Mass. One of the finest of the American Volunteers in the French Army. A graduate of Harvard, and a writer of much talent, he enlisted in the Legion in January, 1915, and was killed in the storming of the Bois Sabot (Champagne); September 28, 1915. He was posthumously awarded the *Médaille Militaire* and the *Croix de Guerre,* and his letters, written home from France, were published in a memorial volume.

Hadley, Ernest. An English volunteer, who was badly wounded in the hand by a shrapnel ball in December, 1914, near Craonnelle. One finger had to be amputated, and his hand was left crippled, incapacitating Hadley for further service.

Hall, Bert, a genial adventurer from Higginsville, Mo., and elsewhere. He returned to America early in 1917, and signed his name to a very readable book, entitled "En l'Air," in which he says of Kiffin Rockwell:

"One of the best of *them* all was poor Kiffin Rockwell, brother of Paul, one of the cleanest, squarest men I ever knew. Kiffin didn't know the meaning of fear. I think he had as many combats in the air as any man in the French aviation. He was credited with three Boches, but I am sure he brought down more, no less than six. . . . Kiffin lost his life in a combat near where he brought down his first

German. He wore the *Médaille Militaire,* the *Croix de Guerre,* and had the rank of sub-lieutenant. I still miss him, and always will, and I have not yet finished revenging Kiffin's loss. He was so skinny, I used to call him the Living Hall Tree. We used to tell Kiffin that if he could keep side on to a German it would be impossible to hit him."

Happe, Captain. One of the most famous of the earlier chiefs of French aviation. His bombing raids into German territory were celebrated throughout the Allied Armies, and his own hairbreadth escapes were countless. Happe never sent his pilots anywhere he would not go himself, but he lost so many men that finally he was sent back to the infantry, and ended the war commanding a Battalion of Colonial Sharpshooters.

Hill, Dudley Lawrence, of Peekskill, N. Y. Hill deserved great credit for flying, as he had defective vision in one eye. He started the war as an ambulance driver, but quickly tired of a non-combatant's part, and was one of the early men to enlist in the Aviation. He ended the war a captain in the United States Air Service.

Hill was decorated with the *Croix de Guerre,* and in December, 1924, was awarded the Cross of the Legion of Honor.

Hubmajer, a broad-shouldered, six-foot-two Serbian Volunteer, who was covered with scars from wounds received in Balkan campaigns, in spite of being under twenty-five years old. He returned to the Serbian Army, in the fall of 1915.

Jim—James Rogers McConnell, of Carthage, North Carolina, after Victor Chapman, Kiffin Rockwell's closest friend in the *Escadrille Américaine.* A graduate of the University of Virginia, and a writer of note, McConnell came to France at the beginning of 1915, and engaged in the Ambulance service, but, to quote his own words, "all along I had been convinced that the United States ought to aid in the struggle against Germany. With that conviction, it was plainly up to me to do more than drive an ambulance. The more I saw of the splendor of the fight the French were making, the more I felt like an *embusqué*—what the British call a "shirker." So I made up my mind to go into aviation."

McConnell liked to write. He had a natural and easy style, and his book "Flying for France" was one of the best war books written;

it was published a few weeks before Jim's death, and was very widely read. Jim McConnell was killed in aerial combat on March 19, 1917; near Flavy-le-Martel (Aisne) his aëroplane falling within the enemy lines. The Germans were retreating from that part of the front, but took time to strip Jim's body and rob it of all identification papers and other effects. French cavalrymen found the wrecked aëroplane, with the remains of its pilot lying near by, three days later, and buried poor Jim where he fell.

McConnell had been decorated with the *Croix de Guerre*, with two citations, and was posthumously awarded the *Médaille Militaire*.

Johnson, Charles Chouteau, of St. Louis, Mo. One of the early members of the *Escadrille Américaine*. He won the *Croix de Guerre* by his good work, and later transferred to the United States Aviation Service, with the rank of Captain.

It is interesting to note that one of Johnson's uncles, Pierre Chouteau, was an American volunteer in the Foreign Legion during the Franco-Prussian War of 1870.

Kelly, Russell, of New York. Kelly's body was never found, and just how he met his death on June 16th, or 17th, 1915, may never be known, as few of his comrades survived that attack. His letters to his family were published, under the title "Kelly of the Foreign Legion." He was posthumously awarded the *Médaille Militaire* and the *Croix de Guerre*.

King, David, of Providence, R. I. King won the *Croix de Guerre*, fighting under the French flag, and later became an officer in the United States Army.

Krogh, Baron Henri L. von Krogh, a Norwegian volunteer, invalided out of the Legion, because of heart trouble, in the fall of 1915.

De Laage, Lieutenant, Alfred de Laage de Meux, second in command of the *Escadrille Américaine* (Escadrille Lafayette). There probably never was an officer more loved and respected by his men than Lieutenant de Laage. He had served in the 14th Regiment of Dragoons, from the outbreak of the war until he was wounded. After recovery from his wound, he entered the Aviation Service, accompanied by his faithful orderly, Jean Drossy, who had saved his life upon the battlefield.

Lieutenant de Laage had already had considerable experience flying at the front, when he and Captain Thénault took charge of the newly formed *Escadrille Américaine,* in April, 1916. Norman Hall says of him in the "Official History of the Lafayette Flying Corps": "He represented all that is best in French character and had a power of personal magnetism which made him a natural leader. He gave to his pilots a new conception of the meaning of patriotism, and it is not the least exaggeration to say that the love which the Americans had for him bordered upon adoration."

He was Kiffin Rockwell's usual flying companion. Kiffin told the following story of one of their sorties together:

"Very early one morning Lieutenant de Laage and I went on patrol together. Over Étain, I saw a Boche underneath me. I immediately dove on him, and when I was just about ready to open fire, two other Germans, whom I had not seen, attacked me, filling my machine full of holes. I thought that my last hour had surely come. Lieutenant de Laage had already had a combat and his machine-gun was jammed. But although it was impossible for him to fire even one shot, he dove on the two Boches who were trying to bring me down and drove them away. I am certain that at that moment he saved my life, as he had done many times before."

After having been five times cited in Army Orders, and winning the *Légion d'Honneur* and the *Croix de Guerre,* Lieutenant de Laage de Meux was killed at Ham (Somme), on May 23, 1917, in a flying accident, as he was leaving his aviation field for a patrol over the Lines. His orderly, Drossy, had been killed exactly one month previously, on April 23rd, accompanying Ronald Hoskier in a two-seater aëroplane as machine-gunner.

Lufbery, Gervais Raoul, of Wallingford, Conn. The "Ace of Aces" of all American aviators. After twenty-nine years of life crammed full of travel and fascinating adventure, Lufbery enlisted in the Foreign Legion in August 1914, and was immediately transferred to the Aviation Service. He began his career as pilot of a fighting aëroplane, when he joined the *Escadrille Américaine* at the Verdun front, having hitherto flown only bombing and observation machines.

APPENDIX

Lufbery destroyed something like fifty German aëroplanes, seventeen of his victories being officially confirmed; he was cited ten times in French Army Orders, and was decorated with the *Légion d'Honneur,* the *Médaille Militaire,* the *Croix de Guerre* with ten palms, and the British Military Medal. He transferred to the United States Air Service, with the rank of Major, on January 1, 1918, and was killed in aërial combat at Maron (Merthe-et-Moselle), on May 19, 1918, his body falling in the garden of a peasant woman's house.

McConnell, James Rogers (See Jim).

Masson, Didier. A French pilot, who had flown in the United States and Mexico before the war. An excellent pilot, he won the *Médaille Militaire* and the *Croix de Guerre* with two palms, and ended the war as a flying instructor at Camp d'Avord.

Morlae, Edward. Claimed to be from California. He deserted from the Legion in October, 1915, returned to America, and signed his name to magazine articles and a book, purporting to tell of his experiences while fighting in France.

Musgrave, Frank, of San Antonio, Texas. A lawyer before the war, Musgrave became famous throughout the Legion as "Lucky Frank," because of his many narrow escapes from death at the front. He transferred to the 170th French Line Regiment, after the Champagne offensive of September-October, 1915, and was captured with his entire company by the Germans near Vaux (Verdun), February 26th, 1916. He remained in German prison camps for the rest of the war, the privations he suffered there greatly undermining his health.

Navarre. The first great French "Ace," and one of the most popular and skilled aviators. He was killed in a flying accident after the war.

Nilson, Elov. A Swedish volunteer, killed in the Somme, September 12, 1916, after winning the *Croix de Guerre,* and being proposed for the *Médaille Militaire.*

Noel, E. Percy. Chicago *Daily News* aviation correspondent in Paris during the war.

Pavelka, Paul, of Madison, Conn. Pavelka joined the *Escadrille Américaine* at the front, only a few days before Kiffin Rockwell was killed. On one of his first flights over the Verdun front, his aëroplane took fire while high in the air, but by careful piloting, Pavelka was able to land safely in a swamp. He declared this experience to be more dreadful than anything he had undergone in the Legion.

Pavelka felt lonely in France, after Kiffin Rockwell fell, and in December, 1916, asked to be sent to the Salonica front. There he became widely and favorably known throughout the Allied Armies, and was awarded the *Croix de Guerre*, with this citation:

"Sujet américain, engagé volontaire pour la durée de la guerre. Grièvement blessé dans l'Infanterie le 16 Juin, 1915. Passé dans l'aviation, est devenu un pilote de chasse ardent, opiniâtre et d'une grande conscience. Ne cesse de donner en Orient des preuves d'allant et de dévouement.

"Nombreux combats à la suite desquels il est rentré fréquemment avec des balles dans son appareil.

(Signé) SARRAIL."

Translation: An American citizen, who volunteered for the duration of the war. Badly wounded as an Infantryman, June 16th, 1915. Transferred to the Aviation, where he has become a keen fighting pilot, being tenacious and very conscientious. While in the Near East he has always been on the go, giving untiring proof of devotion to duty. Has fought numerous air duels, from which he has often returned with his machine riddled by bullets.

Pavelka's death was a curious instance of the irony of fate. After his countless narrow escapes as an Infantryman and as an aviator, he was killed by a fall from a horse, a misfortune which might have befallen him when he was a boy on the farm in Connecticut! One day, while off duty near Salonica, he ran across an English cavalryman, a former friend in the Legion. Pavelka visited his old comrade at the latter's regimental headquarters, and while trying to ride a notoriously vicious horse, was thrown, trampled on, and fatally injured. He died the following day, November 12, 1917, and was given an imposing funeral, officers and men from all the Allied Armies in the Near East being present. Edgar Bouligny, one of Pavelka's close American friends in the Legion, and who also had changed to the Aviation after wounds, arrived at Salonica just in time to learn of his death and attend his funeral.

Pechkoff, Zinovi. A Russian volunteer, adopted son of the famous writer, Maxim Gorky. His right arm was shot away at the shoulder May 9, 1915, but in spite of this disability, he remained in the service of France. In 1916, and again in 1918, he was sent to the United States on lecture tours, and after the Armistice, he was attached to Kolchak's, Denikin's and Wrangel's White Armies, in their efforts to rescue Russia from the Bolshevists.

In January, 1925, Pechkoff was a captain commanding a company of the Fourth Foreign Regiment, in Morocco. He was decorated with the *Légion d'Honneur, Médaille Militaire, Croix de Guerre,* and several Russian and other Allied medals.

Phelizot, René, of Chicago, Ill. He ran away from home at the age of thirteen, and was first a cabin-boy on a Mississippi river passenger boat, later seeking adventure in many lands. Phelizot's father was of French origin, and being in Paris, resting after a long big game shooting excursion in the African jungles, René enlisted in the Foreign Legion soon after war was declared, in August, 1914. He made an excellent and cheerful soldier. Phelizot died in the military hospital at Fismes (Marne), March 9, 1915.

Prince, Charles. Uncle of Norman Prince, and for many years a resident of France. Known as "Uncle Charlie" to the American Volunteers in the French Aviation and the Foreign Legion, because of his affectionate interest in them.

Prince, Norman, of Pride's Crossing, Mass. A Harvard graduate, Prince had flown much in America before the war. He came to France early in 1915, and on March 4th enlisted in the Aviation Service, and entered the training school at Pau. Prince worked long and faithfully at forming an escadrille composed of American Volunteer aviators, and was one of the original members of the *Escadrille Américaine.* He was fatally injured October 12, 1916, when his aëroplane crashed during a night landing, after protecting one of Captain Happe's bombing raids across the Rhine.

Norman Prince was named sous-lieutenant, and decorated with the *Légion d'Honneur,* as he lay on his deathbed; he had previously been awarded the *Médaille Militaire* and the *Croix de Guerre.* He died October 15, 1916. A memorial volume was published of his letters from the front.

Rapier. An English volunteer, who became a sergeant in the Legion. He was invalided out of service in 1915.

Rumsey, Lawrence, of Buffalo, N. Y. One of the early members of the *Escadrille Américaine*. Ill-health kept him from doing much actual flying.

Scanlan, Lawrence, of Cedarhurst, Long Island. He remained in hospital for almost a year and a half after his wound of June 16, 1915, and was decorated with the *Croix de Guerre* while still under the surgeon's care, for his courage in action. Invalided out of the army at the end of 1916, with one leg six inches shorter than the other, he re-enlisted in the Aviation a few days later. After several months of training, he was forced to give up flying.

Scanlan died from his wound, Nov. 25, 1920; he was operated on eight times during the month preceding his death, and his crippled leg was amputated, but too late to save his life.

Seeger, Alan, of New York City. The famous poet of the Foreign Legion, he wrote some of the most beautiful verse inspired by the war. Seeger was killed during the storming of Belloy-en-Santerre (Somme), July 4th, 1916, and was posthumously awarded the *Médaille Militaire* and the *Croix de Guerre*. His War Letters, Diary and Poems were published in two volumes, and also translated into French.

Smith, John. The name under which John Earle Fike, of Wooster, Ohio, enlisted in the Foreign Legion. He was killed June 16th, 1915, and his body was never found.

Soubiran, Robert, of New York City. He was born in France, of French parentage, but emigrated to the United States at an early age. When war broke out in 1914, Soubiran heeded the call of his mother country, came to France, and joined the Legion. He was wounded during the Champagne attack, October, 1915, and later transferred to the Aviation. He was decorated with the *Légion d'Honneur* and the *Croix de Guerre,* and ended the war a captain in the United States Aviation Service.

Térésien, Sergeant of the *Section* of C Battalion, Second Marching Regiment of the Second Foreign Regiment, in which were most of the American Volunteers. His left arm was shot away in

Champagne, September 25, 1915.

Thaw, William, of Pittsburg, Pa. Thaw ended the war a lieutenant-colonel in the United States Aviation Service, after having officially destroyed five German aëroplanes. He became an officer of the *Légion d'Honneur,* won the *Croix de Guerre* with four palms and two stars, and the Distinguished Service Cross with bronze oak leaf.

Thénault, Georges. Captain commanding the *Escadrille Américaine* (Escadrille Lafayette) from the day it was organized until it was disbanded, Jan. 1, 1918, and its American pilots were taken over by the United States aviation service. Thénault was a French army flyer before the war, and was selected to lead the American Volunteer Pilots, because of his excellent record as chief of a French escadrille at the front.

Thénault's task as commanding officer of the *Escadrille Américaine* was a difficult one. He was instructed by the French Ministry of War and the Minister of Foreign Affairs, on taking charge of the Escadrille, not to be too strict with his men, because they were foreign volunteers. He was not much older than some of his pilots, but his ripe experience as a peace time and war flyer enabled him to acquit himself of his task with distinction. He performed his duties with tact and kindly interest in his men, few of whom fortunately tried to take, advantage of the orders he had received not to over-discipline them.

Captain Thénault was decorated with the *Légion d'Honneur* and the *Croix de Guerre,* with four palms. After the war, he wrote and published a book: "The Story of the Lafayette Escadrille." He was Military Attaché for Aëronautics at the French Embassy, Washington, in January, 1925.

Thorin, Daniel William. "Billy" Thorin was born in Sweden, but went to America when very young, and became a United States citizen. He recovered from his wounds received in Champagne, September 28, 1915, and rejoined the Legion at the front, but after a few months contracted tuberculosis. After a long stay in hospital, he was invalided out of the army, and returned to America. Mr. John Jay Chapman sent him to a sanatorium in Arizona, where he died, September 25, 1918. "Billy's" last request was that he be given a military funeral and this wish was complied with, the Governor of Arizona sending a regiment of troops to escort the Legionnaire's remains to their final resting place.

Trinkard, Charles, of Ozone Park, N. Y. Was shot through the shoulder, September 28, 1915, when the Legion stormed the Bois Sabot. Transferred to the Aviation in March, 1917, and was killed in a flying accident, Thanksgiving Day, November 29th, 1917. He had just returned from a patrol over the lines, and started to do some acrobatic stunts over a village, where he knew his old comrades of the Legion were quartered. He wing-slipped while making a vertical turn and, because of the low altitude at which he was flying, crashed into the ground before he could regain speed, and was instantly killed. Some of his American Legionnaire friends were the first to reach his wrecked machine, and Christopher Charles wrote later:

"We did not know who had fallen, but when we saw the khaki uniform and the red *fourragère* of the Legion we were mightily grieved, for we all knew Trink and the splendid work he had done as an infantryman. He did more than his duty in this war and did it cheerfully."

Weeks, Kenneth, of New Bedford, Mass. His body was found between the lines, in November, 1915, over five months after he was killed. Kenneth Weeks' War Letters were published in book form, and he was posthumously awarded the *Médaille Militaire* and the *Croix de Guerre.*

Zinn, Frederick William, of Battle Creek, Mich. He transferred to the Aviation, after having been wounded in Champagne, October, 1915. He specialized in aërial photography, and his months of experience doing this work at the front caused him to be one of the first American aviators in the French service to be asked for by the United States Air Service, after the entry of America into the war. Zinn was decorated with the *Croix de Guerre* for his conduct at the front with the French Aviation Corps. He ended the war a Major in the A. E. F.

GLOSSARY

(Kiffin Rockwell frequently used French military terms in his letters; instead of translating them, they have been italicized.)

Appareil: machine, aëroplane.

Appel: roll-call.

"Aux armes": "To arms."

Amateur: aviator.

"Bébé" or *"Baby":* pet name given by the combat-machine pilots to the little monoplane Nieuport aëroplane.

Brevet militaire: military flying license.

Bon: abbreviation for *bataillon;* a full French regiment is composed of four battalions.

Casque: here means fur-lined leather head-dress worn by aviators when flying.

Cie. : abbreviation for *compagnie;* there are four companies in a French battalion, each commanded by a captain.

Consigne: formal instruction given to a sentinel; also the punishment of confinement to barracks.

Consultation motivée: justifiable reporting to sick-call.

Croix de Guerre: War Cross, awarded with a citation in army orders.

Déjeuner: luncheon; *petit dejeuner:* breakfast.

2ème classe (deuxième classe soldat): "buck private."

GLOSSARY

Division Marocain: one of the finest divisions in the French Colonial Army, composed during the World War of the Foreign Legion, a regiment of Zouaves and one of Algerian sharp-shooters, with batteries of field artillery.

Élève pilote: student-pilot.

Épreuve: trial flight for flying license.

Escouade (abbreviated *Escde.*): smallest unit in a French regiment, commanded by a corporal; there are four *escouades* in a *section.*

Exempt service: exempted from military duties, usually by doctor's order.

Gamelle, la: metal bowl from which French soldiers eat; the old Legion corporals and sergeants, disgusted at the awkwardness of the Volunteers for the World War, sometimes taunted them by saying that they had enlisted for *"la gamelle,"* or the French army ration.

"Garde à vous": "Be on your guard," "Danger."

Légion d'Honneur: the highest French decoration awarded to officers in time of war. Also given in time of peace for distinguished services to France.

Légion Étrangère: Foreign Legion.

Mécanicien: mechanic.

Médaille Militaire: the highest decoration privates and under-officers in the French army can win on the battlefield. It is also given to generals commanding an army for conspicuous gallantry.

Militaire: military; also, a soldier; used in Kiffin Rockwell's letters in the sense of militaire discipline.

Mitrailleuse: rapid-fire, or machine-gun.

Passe-montagne: knitted woollen bonnet worn over the head during cold weather; it also protects the ears and neck.

Petit poste: outpost nearest the enemy.

Popote: mess.

Poste de police: guard house.

Réclamer: to protest.

Réformer: to invalid out of the army.

GLOSSARY

Repos: rest, "break ranks."

Réserve général: reserve depot for pilots and aëroplanes, from which the escadrilles at the front were supplied.

Son: abbreviation for *section.* A company in the French army is composed of four sections, each commanded by a sergeant.

Soupe ("la soupe"): call to meals in the French army; also means the army ration.

Vaguemestre: regiment al postmaster.

www.ingramcontent.com/pod-product-compliance
Lightning Source LLC
Chambersburg PA
CBHW030937150426
42812CB00064B/2988/J